AF553454

Housing on the Hills in India

About the Author

Bhaskar Majumder (B. 1956) obtained his M.A., M. Phil. and Ph. D. Degrees in Economics from the University of Calcutta. With the credit of teaching experience for many years in various Colleges of Calcutta, he is presently working as Professor of Economics in G.B. Pant Social Science Institute, Allahabad. He has contribution of publishing eight books and sixty one research papers besides completing twelve research projects supported by Planning Commission, ICSSAR, World Bank and NTPC, etc. He had been a visiting fellow at M.S.H., Paris in 2004 and is visiting faculty at Malaviya Centre For Research, Banaras Hindu University since 2006.

Housing on the Hills in India

Bhaskar Majumder

CONCEPT PUBLISHING COMPANY PVT. LTD.
NEW DELHI-110059

ISBN-13: 978-81-8069-742-5

First Published 2011

Published and Printed by

Concept Publishing Company Pvt. Ltd.
Regd. Office:
A/15-16, Commercial Block, Mohan Garden
New Delhi-110059 (India)
Phones : 25351460, 25351794,
Fax : 091-11-25357109
Email : publishing@conceptpub.com
Website: www.conceptpub.com

Editorial Office:
H-13, Bali Nagar, New Delhi-110 015, India

Cataloging in Publication Data--*Courtesy:* D.K. Agencies (P) Ltd. <docinfo@dkagencies.com>

Majumder, Bhaskar.
Housing on the hills in India / Bhaskar Majumder.
p. cm.
Includes bibliographical references (p.) and index.
ISBN 9788180697425

1. Housing, Rural--India--Uttarakhand. 2. Housing policy--India--Uttarakhand. 3. Rural development projects--India--Uttarakhand. I. Title.

DDC 363.5095451 22

Preface

In this book, 'rural housing' connotes dwelling units plus a support system such as approach roads, a water supply system, sewage and garbage disposal systems, electricity and fuel, facilities such as markets, health institutions, and public space. In this book, we have looked into the adequacy of living space per person, and the quality and durability of rural houses in existence. We have covered houses constructed under Government schemes, particularly under Indira Awaas Yojana (IAY), as well as houses privately constructed in rural areas. Government-supported houses have been seen in two categories, i.e., houses for the BPL households and those for general (non-BPL) households. We have studied the existence of and scope for availability of water, kitchens, toilets, and common resources in rural housing provisions. In case of state-supported housing, we have also explored the mode of payment of aid sanctioned by the Government and aid actually received by the households. Basically, we have examined the role of rural housing for decent living of population rooted in rural Uttarakhand.

What we have proposed in this book is that execution of rural housing schemes ensures utilization of local resources, including manpower, and simultaneously promotes rural infrastructure; it uplifts the housing condition and ensures security of the rural income-poor people settled in rural hilly regions of the state; it may discourage forced migration of rural people.

The empirical basis of the proposition was the rural region of Uttarakhand in India. The book establishes that rural housing as a means of living ensures not only safe and comfortable living of the rural population, but also stops forced migration of people. The employment response of planned rural housing may retain rural population within the rural region. An income-poor family can afford to spend an insignificant proportion of its income on housing over the other basic needs of life, like food and clothing. This is because there is a lower cost threshold below which a most modest acceptable housing provision cannot be ensured. If there is a sizeable section of the rural population who is income-poor, then low-cost rural housing is one of the means of social security for them. Low-cost rural housing uses local raw materials available often free of cost and manpower for such constructions. The utilization of local manpower may also signal if there had been any diffusion of technology through Government initiatives in constructing houses. Investment in housing by the Government for the income-poor families can improve the living and working conditions of low-income families, stop forced migration by increasing the opportunities for local employment by linkages with other development schemes of the Government and stimulate the development of other sectors of the economy. This occurs by safe existence and stability of the households via housing and optimizing the time in productive uses. Planning for rural housing by uses of local materials, labour, and credit shows the avenues for not only the utilization of local resources that otherwise would have remained idle, but also saving scarce resources of the economy for alternative uses.

The households at the peak of the hills were affected most by natural calamity followed by those at the middle part and valley. The major calamities faced by households included earthquake, fire (forest), landslide, snowfall, river sliding and rainfall. Crack in house was reported because of landslide and earthquake. House burnt was explained only by domestic fire. Death of animals was explained by twin factors, fire and earthquake. Falling down of house was explained mostly by snowfall, rainfall, earthquake and landslide. Most of the beneficiary households under housing programme reported that they were not benefited from other development programmes.

We found positive impact of housing on overall livelihood of households. Because of housing, the households felt protected against natural calamities and wild animals and they could save money for the education of their children, overcome seasonal difficulties and search for employment opportunities. While the correlation coefficient between selected indicators increased after implementation of housing programme, it had exceptions for two indicators, one being uses of Common Property Resources and the other being employment opportunities. The perception of the households regarding impact of housing on the livelihood of households centered mainly on safety from rainwater, shelter by having RCC roof, adequate rooms for members in family and other feelings like owning a house, self-satisfaction, safety from adverse weather, improved family honour etc.

The houses on the hills in Uttarakhand had 'no uniform pattern' and location. In case the households in the glacier got the chance to construct a house in a village located lower in altitude, they would prefer it there rather than remaining in the glacier.

In the remote hills, most of the households were homogeneous by culture. Not much intervention by the government so far helped maintain this homogeneity. Locally settled households were engaged in every kind of work across social categories. Economic categories were yet to get sharpened. Hence, there was social accommodation by community life and limited economic inequality.

While construction and living in privately owned house

remain in the private domain, the location of the house shows space under the jurisdiction of the state. Hence, apart from provision of houses for the income-poor, the state may have reasons to intervene in housing by planning and settlement of households and relocation if and when necessary.

The book offers the following recommendations:

Households should be prevented from constructing their houses in dangerous places like earthquake-prone zones. There has to be a sensible rehabilitation policy in case a particular zone is declared earthquake-prone where people are already settled. No housing for settlement of households should be allowed above 15,000 ft. for natural safety of the households and protection of nature. The hilly zone above this specified height should be the 'natural zone' reserved/ preserved by the state. The argument for *pucca* (concrete) house generally may not be the only solution for living by households on the hills at different altitudes. The type of the house on the range of hills will depend more on the climatic conditions and natural slopes than on the conventional indicators like safety and security. Often the semi-*pucca* houses made of wood and boulder as components of wall, tin/slate as component of roof, and clay for floor may be more acceptable and climate-friendly for the households relative to conventional concrete (*pucca*) houses. The choice has to be left to the households for these components of house. The roof of the residential house preferably will be conic in case it is located on the top because of snow fall while it may be flat when the altitude at which the house is located is much lower. On the areas adjacent to dense forests the house has to be more than one-storey building to remain protected from wild animals while at the bottom of the hills it may be single storey depending on the requirement of family members and domestic animals. In case the target households own land where they construct residential house, the state has to look into the general drainage and sewerage system before allowing construction of the house under the housing schemes. In case the target households like the widow of military personnel killed in war, and physically challenged persons do not own land, the location has to be decided by the state in agreement with the beneficiary household, so as to ensure public facilities like water, electricity, drainage/sewerage, health-related facilities, educational institutions, transport, and market. Following the natural voluntary division of the large household into a number of nuclear families, the right to being enlisted in BPL should not be automatically ensured. In such cases, the offshoot nuclear household may be suggested to go for credit-cum-subsidy scheme. The norm fixed at 20 sq. mt. as construction area has to be relaxed depending on the altitude, transportation cost and availability of natural safe space. The implementing authorities should guide the target households to use local materials and cost-effective disaster resistant and environment-friendly technologies. The implementing authorities should contact organizations and institutions for information on suitable building materials, designs and methods to help the households in the construction of durable and cost-effective houses. This will also lead to training-cum-information sharing of the households considered as beneficiaries under housing. The basic information like BPL list, permanent wait list of households for housing programme, list of disaster-resistant construction, Family Register, details of households benefited by other development programmes must be available in each Gram Panchayat office.

The Gram Panchayat has to certify the BPL list prepared by the competent authority and has to follow the list while selecting households as target beneficiaries; convene open meetings of Gram Sabha and enlist names of shelterless households, widows, physically and mentally challenged people, in addition to the pre-fixed quota for SCs and STs; organize awareness campaign each year so far as construction of houses is concerned for the safety and security of the households, and prepare permanent wait list on an annual basis and send it to Block office and DRDA for their acceptance. In addition, the Panchayat should include poor non-SC/ST households in case the region does not have adequate number of SC/ST households. The Panchayat has to assess every year the condition and durability of the houses constructed under housing schemes and suggest measures accordingly for upgradation of the house and guide the households for temporary relocation. The Panchayat should take the responsibilities for marketing of local agro-based, forest-based and household industry products produced by income-poor household-entrepreneurs, particularly women, to provide them income support. In case of forestry-based products, there has to be a joint responsibility by a trio : the entrepreneur-household, the Gram Panchayat and the Forest Department to ensure participation in replenishment of forestry on a planned time span, once forest resources are allowed to be converted into individual products. The Gram Panchayats should promote construction of traditional houses that we found more acceptable to the households without any compromise with safety and security of the households. The Gram Panchayat should enlist the permanent address of the specified households in case of double settlement of households on the hills. In case of landless, assetless and incomeless households, Gram Sabha land has to be provided for his housing and compulsion of land ownership has to be withdrawn from housing schemes.

The state government has to allow the beneficiary households to take sand and wood from the concerned departments at subsidized rates. The state government has to strengthen the PRIs by assigning them more rights and responsibilities like organizing awareness programmes regarding safe housing, monitoring and supervision of implementation of the housing schemes. The state government has to link housing schemes with other on-going welfare-cum-development schemes in the state. The state government should develop and launch an integrated training programme for representatives of Gram Panchayats and settled households that have to cover all aspects of disaster management. The state government should empower Gram Panchayats with amending the permanent wait list in his jurisdiction on an annual basis. Provision of reservation should be based on ratio of caste/class of permanent wait list or the number of BPL households in the Gram Panchayats. The state government should develop 'model house' based on location, tradition of the locality, household requirements, safety and security, climate and calamity. The enlisted and selected households should be given the choice to select one model from the module box following which the money will be sanctioned. The government has already made the provision of supplying construction materials to beneficiary households at controlled price. However, based on our non-observation of any household availing this facility and also based on high transport cost on the hills, the responsibility of arranging construction materials for sale at subsidized prices at a particular zone has to be ensured by the block level officials. In view of the cheap usable cement blocks for construction of walls defining perimeter of the house by plinth area, the use by more of such techniques by other households should be encouraged by the government. The responsibility for dissemination of this knowledge has to be executed through the block officials or NGOs/SHGs and supported by the GP. The state government has a regular policy of rehabilitating households in distress following natural calamities that has to continue by schemes like Prime Minister's Relief Fund, and State Relief Fund. The state government has to form vigilance committee at multiple levels like village, block and district to look into the grievance of the households that they may face in getting their names enlisted for housing benefits up to getting money released for the said purpose. The details about this committee by names of members and assigned duties have to be displayed in public places and a register maintained by the concerned office for redressal of grievances.

The construction of private toilet for use should not be a part of housing programme. The question should be left to Total Sanitation Programme. The installation of smokeless stove as an integral component of IAY should be withdrawn. Instead, the government should provide option to beneficiary households to take LPG connections at subsidized rate for the hills. Since, wood happens to be the main fuel for the households on the hills, hence, there has to be replenishment of wood as a source of fuel by joint forest management approach rather than stopping the households from using wood as a fuel for cooking.

All the concerned officials in the Government should be made aware of the rule that the Gram Sabha is the final authority for selection and approval of the beneficiary and that no further approval is required by any other authority.

Generally, Credit cum - Subsidy Scheme (CCSS) fails when the IAY offers 'money gift' for housing. The not-so-poor also do not have much idea about the CCS Scheme. This awareness may be generated by the Panchayat/state government so that the households above the margin or in the wait list with remote chance to get IAY house may be persuaded to go for CCS Scheme.

The book is an offshoot of the research report that I submitted to the Planning Commission, Government of India, on 'Impact of Rural Housing Programmes on People Settled in Rural Uttarakhand : A Study'. I express my sincere thanks to Sri. V.K. Bhatia, Adviser (SER) of Planning Commission, Sri D.K. Mustafi, the-then Dy. Secretary to GOI and Sri B.S. Rathor, SRO (SER) for smooth running of the Project by financial and time support. I also express my sincere thanks to Sri S. Mukherjee, Dy. Secretary (SER).

I got all the support for collection of information from

the District Magistrates and CDOs of all selected districts and equally from DDOs, PDs, BDOs, Panchayat Secretaries, and Gram Pradhans.

I express my sincere thanks to Prof. Pradeep Bhargawa, Director of the Institute, who silently provided all the necessary support to give the report a shape as it is now. I express my sincere thanks to those academicians and activists who provided me insights.

I express my sincere thanks to Mousumi Majumder who took the pain to set the manuscript in order. My relatives at both Kolkata and Delhi deserve mention for their love and blessings in my academic efforts.

It goes without saying the members in my research team, namely M.G. Gupta, G.N. Jha, S.K. Jaiswal, deserve special mention for shouldering the responsibilities in collecting field data and in analysis.

Allahabad **Bhaskar Majumder**
March, 2010

Contents

List of Tables

List of Boxes

List of Abbreviations

APL	Above Poverty Line
BPL	Below Poverty Line
CCSS	Credit-cum-Subsidy Scheme
DRDA	District Rural Development Authority
IAY	Indira Awaas Yojana
JRY	Jawahar Rozgar Yojana
NHP	National Housing Policy
MNP	Minimum Needs Programme
BAY	Bhuskhalan Awaas Yojana
UAY	Uttarakhand Awaas Yojana
NSSO	National Sample Survey Organization
CPRs	Common Property Resources
PRIs	Panchayati Raj Institutions
EWS	Economically Weaker Sections
PMGSY	Pradhan Mantri Gramodaya Yojana
NREP	National Rural Employment Programme
RLEGP	Rural Landless Employment Guarantee Programme
GOI	Government of India
FPSs	Fair Price Shops
ILO	International Labour Organization
NHB	National Housing Bank
HUDCO	Housing Urban Development Corporation
GIC	General Insurance Company
NGOs	Non-Governmental Organizations
UT	Union Territories
STs	Scheduled Tribes
SCs	Scheduled Castes
OBCs	Other Backward Classes
RHP	Rural Housing Policy

List of Flow Charts

1

Rural Housing : An Overview

1.1 Housing : The Concept and the Components

A need is felt as basic when its absence endangers the very survival of the individual. The physical expression of any need is a usable product or service. Naturally, such needs include food first and then shelter. While consumption of food protects the biological existence of the individual, shelter protects her from adverse nature and fear associated with both controllable and apparently uncontrollable forces that are external to the individual concerned. These forces include fire, cyclone, rain, flood, earthquake, adverse weather, and insects. Ownership of house also ensures the identity, self-esteem, and privacy of the individual and enhances the scope for participation in society. Housing also promotes a family life and facilitates a social and cultural life for the individual.

Housing is one of the major components of basic needs that offer the individuals and families privacy and security for living. The protection of individuals and families is dependent directly on the type of shelter they have. The creativity and competence of individuals is also dependent directly on where they are, that is, where they live. Participation in social festivals, and cultural programmes organized by communities also depends on the stable living of the individuals in families in houses. The sense of social identity of individuals is linked very much with the kind of location-cum-addresses the individuals have. All these aspects are essentially components of decent conditions of human living. Thus, we see rural housing as a major component of basic needs of human life.

The basic questions related to what is rural have been explained elsewhere (Hodge and Whitby, 1981, pp. 4-5). It may be characterized by existence and functioning of local governments, it may be by size of human settlements; it may be by indicators like occupational structure, and landholding. There may also be functional categories of villages like those that are linked more with urban areas, those that are linked only with sub-urban areas, that are intermediate, and those that are extremely rural.

The term 'rural housing' is used to connote dwelling units plus utility services such as approach roads, a water supply system, sewage and garbage disposal systems, electricity and fuel, facilities such as markets, health and centres. In the literature on housing, the distinction between 'push' and 'pull' factors are known. Push factors work when the rural population has low landholding per capita as a productive asset, low productivity, and hence suffer from income-poverty. Pull factors work when social and economic opportunities in urban life attract population from the countryside (Wakely, Schmetzer, and Mumtaz, 1976, p. 3). Some of the push factors may be conspicuous by their absence, which are present in the urban regions, e.g, health care and education. After a point, thus, the distinction between pull and push factors becomes blurred.

It may not be that all the facilities associated with rural housing can be ensured in one stroke. However, the minimum necessary investment in housing can improve the living and working conditions of low-income households, increase employment in housing-related public works, and stimulate the development of other sectors of the economy. This occurs both by increasing the demand of their products and by improving the productivity of the work force (UN, 1978, p. 33).

We describe 'housing' by the services 'housing' is supposed to provide. It is a universal proposition that 'housing' provides services, but the kind of services may vary depending on ownership of houses by income-rich and income-poor, in rich and poor countries, and in varied locations and circumstances. As such, by services taken as indices to describe housing, housing remains a heterogeneous product.

The UN Habitat Conference, 1976, focused on the inextricability of housing from the environment. This 'environment' includes both the natural and man-made facilities and obstructions around people, like water supply, waste disposal facilities, etc. (Burns and Grebler, 1977, pp. 15-16). Housing accommodates a family that survives as a biological unit and protects itself against various climatic conditions and adverse circumstances. Housing is the central location of human life and human settlements. The corollaries that follow include their location in the village, living rooms with privacy, indoor cooking facilities, storage facilities, private sanitation, public sanitation, bathing facilities with privacy, open space adjoining dwelling units for recreation and public meetings, schools and health centres.

1.1.1 Housing as a Physical Space

Housing as a physical space may have both narrow and broad versions. The narrow version concentrates on the dwelling unit of the household with facilities for living available within the boundary of the dwelling unit. The broad version sets the dwelling unit in the context of neighbouring dwelling units, which is the human and ecological environment adjoining the space for living of any particular family. This environment is bounded by a narrow geographic space. We consider the village as the bottom-most unit for selection of this geographic space. We follow the broader version of housing as a physical space.

The ILO Conference, 1953, resolved that 'adequate housing accommodations and related facilities are one of the essentials of a good life, one of the fundamental requirements of an efficient, satisfied labour force, and one of the foundations of satisfactory community life' (Burns and Grebler, 1977, p. 100). The General Assembly adopted the Declaration of the International Development Strategy for the Second UN Development Decade in 1970. The Declaration advised the developing countries to 'take steps to provide improved housing and related community facilities in both the urban and rural areas especially for low-income groups' (Burns and Grebler, 1977, pp. 100-101). Habitat II Conference, 1996, of the UN recognized housing or adequate shelter as a universal human right. '. . . .the right to housing goes beyond the right to a roof over one's head. It includes access to the systems essential to a healthy home : safe water and sanitation, waste disposal, modern energy, transport and proximity to social services' (UNDP, 1998, p. 89).

1.1.2 Housing as an Accommodation : Physical, Social and Psychological

In outward appearance, housing is a homogeneous service provided by a physical space. In essence, housing is much more than a physical space and is anything but homogeneous. For the asset-cum-income poor, it is a shelter for survival of the family. For the destitute, it is a shelter at least for the night. For the people employed in some stable occupations and the middle income groups, it is a space for living in comfort. For the income rich, it is a luxury that demonstrates more than it accommodates the family. For rural houses, it is almost always boundaryless, while for the urban houses it is accompanied by boundaries circumscribing the residential plot of land. For city slums, the houses are boundaryless. There seems to be more social accommodation in case of rural houses relative to urban houses. Housing has not only social attachment but also psychological attachment. The latter involves not only a relation between the neighbours within the bigger boundary, particularly in the rural areas, but also an attachment with local culture, language, rituals, belief, traditions. In a word, all the visible and invisible practices that bind the local people are centered on the living or the housing of the people around whom those practices revolve.

An individual unsettled by compulsion because of absence of any stable address cannot express himself. The implication is need for housing. This also implies a mode of living whereby people can participate in decision-making that affects their lives. Housing as a durable, if not permanent, mode of living ensures not only the safety of the people but also a method whereby people exercise their power in processes of decision-making. Provision of housing also checks demobilization of people in the society. In other words, a strong bondage that houses ensure among households bonds the whole neighbourhood. Extension of the bondage of a particular neighbourhood bonds all the adjoining areas/neighbourhoods. This is where the relevance of housing as a promoter of social expression of individuals comes in.

Rural areas have their natural formations. These formations include cooperation and collective spirit, occasional conflicts and its resolution at the local level. Attempts at urbanization, either through government intervention by extension of service sector-cum-financial institutions, and/or extension of urban/city/metropolitan areas that grab the existing rural areas, lead to injection of non-easily resolvable conflicts. With intervention by the government for poverty alleviation, the scenario has changed towards dependence on external finance and other supports. The consequences in the mindset of rural people from auto centric development to dependent development have also percolated to the housing sector. Thus, though housing remained historically the individual's responsibility for the family or peoples' activity at the collective level, it has changed of late by being more of dependency on government intervention. The landlessness/joblessness/ incomelessness make this dependency for shelter more acute.

1.2 Living Condition of People settled in Rural Regions as Linked with Housing

Historically as people came down from the trees, emerged from the caves, and came out of forests for conversion of nature for purposes of production, they started cleaning forests and land to convert it for cultivation. In parallel, there came the need for housing for living and looking after the area covered for cultivation. This included essentially collective living-cum-cultivation. Houses started being built for protection and collective living and for mutual help and hence there came living in cluster-type houses. These houses obviously used local available materials. The total scenario showed small cluster-type human settlements which were identified as villages. These villages came into being by human settlements based on their searching for other means of livelihood like availability of food, and barriers from others' aggression. For economies today, that are far from industrialized and urbanized, the same mode of collective living persists. Any village in less advanced regions of India show the villages as open space, though not necessarily reflecting collective living. There has come with respect to time stratification by private and public ownership of land and buildings of various types. Hence, the living conditions of people settled in the villages under transition have started changing.

A country like India shows most of the population settled in villages. Not only the number of villages outnumbers the towns but the villages dominate in terms of number of population settled and engagement of most of the village settled population in land-based activities. Human settlements in India by type generally show three types–rural, urban and forest-based. The last-type generally covers the tribal population seen to be outside the mainstream society, mainstream understood by the society subject to the rules and regulations of the Government. We focus on the mainstream society in this book.

Even inside the mainstream rural society and human settlements, we find both concentrated settlements and dispersed settlements based on social, economic and cultural factors. Concentrated settlements are likely to be established with the already existing transport-market facilities, or that the former may lead to the development of the latter. Dispersed settlements may come into being because of a number of reasons, like social segmentation, caste categories, occupations, and access to Common Property Resources (CPRs).

In this book we have examined if rural housing as a space for living ensures not only safe and comfortable living of the rural population, but also stops directionless movement of people. The employment response of planned rural housing may also retain rural population within the rural region. An income-poor family can afford to spend an insignificant proportion of its income on housing over the other necessities of life, like food and clothing. This is because there is a lower cost threshold below which a most modest acceptable housing provision cannot be ensured. If there is a sizeable sec ion of the rural population which is income-poor, then low-cost rural housing is one of the means of social security for them. We are going to see if the construction cost for rural houses per square metre will be much lower relative to that for urban houses. Rural houses are supposed to use local raw materials and family labour for such constructions. The utilization of local hired labourers for construction of houses may also show if there had been any diffusion of technology through Government initiatives in construction of houses. We are going to examine if housing improves the living conditions of low-income families, increase employment and stimulate the income generating activities in the rural regions. We are going to examine how the provision for rural housing cannot only ensure utilization of local natural resources and manpower, but also can release labour potential for alternative productive uses when housing is ensured.

1.3 Housing as a Policy Measure

Housing as a policy measure dates back to the British industrial revolution. Housing as a public measure, however, dates back even before that. '... the work-houses provided under the Elizabethan Poor Laws of 1601, later known as almshouses in the United States as well as in England, served as convenient containers for watching over the needy and perhaps unruly who were given work, fed and clothed, if necessary. In the Mercantilist period, rulers used the inducement of better housing to lure people into urban places specializing in the production of goods for export, one of the principal goals of Mercantilist policy' (Burns and Grebler, 1977, p. 69). It is since the industrial revolution that the questions related to public intervention in housing came to be talked about particularly in the context of the then dominant political-economic ideology of *laissez faire.*

'State intervention in housing in the early twentieth century was in part a response... to the increasing strength of working class militancy.... However, state intervention in housing cannot be seen as resulting only from working class pressure. While the timing and form of the 1919 Housing Act was greatly influenced by working class struggle, it was not a total watershed in the nature of state intervention' (Bedale, 1980, p. 41).

The scheme for allotment of house sites-cum-construction assistance as part of the Minimum Needs Programme in rural areas is under the purview of State sector (GOI, 1995-96, p. 180). The Central Government supplements the efforts of the State Government by implementing some central and centrally sponsored programmes (GOI, 1996-97, p. 192). An early effort for provision of public housing in post-independence India came in the form of social housing schemes introduced during the 1950s (Box 1.1).

Box 1.1: Social Housing Schemes in India, 1950s

Housing Schemes	*Year of Introduction*
Subsidized Housing Scheme	1952
Low Income Group Housing Scheme	1954
Plantation Workers Scheme	1956
Village Housing Project	1957
Middle Income Housing Scheme	1959

Source : GOI, Planning Commission, 1983, Task Force on Housing and Urban Development, Shelter for the Urban Poor and Slum Improvement, September.

By 1974 all the housing schemes, except the one for plantation workers, had been transferred to the State Governments. There was little role of both the Central and State Governments in ensuring the living through housing of the rural poor in India. Even the Task Force of the Planning Commission, GOI, meant for the urban sector, found that the housing schemes have so far benefited only the middle and higher income groups (GOI, Planning Commission, 1983, p. xv).

1.3.1 National Housing Policy, 1994

In India, the National Housing Policy was adopted by the

Parliament in August 1994 (GOI, 1994-95, p. 164). The long-term goals of the Policy were reducing homelessness, improving the housing conditions of the inadequately housed, providing a minimum level of basic services and amenities to all (GOI, 1996, Sept., p. 114). The National Housing Policy, 1994 recognized the importance of both rural and urban housing in the overall development of the poor in both the rural and urban areas (GOI, 1997-98, p. 148).

1.3.2 National Housing and Habitat Policy, 1998

The National Housing and Habitat Policy, 1998 announced by the Government of India aimed at development of housing infrastructure through strong public-private partnership. It aims at ensuring that housing, along with supporting services, is treated as priority sector at par with infrastructure, facilitate construction of dwelling units each year with emphasis on the poor (GOI, 2000-01, p. 206). The 1998 Policy aimed to facilitate the construction of 20 lakh dwelling units each year for the poor covering both urban and rural areas (GOI, 1998-99, p. 153). The Policy recognized the importance of both rural and urban housing in the total development of the rural people and the urban poor (GOI, 1997-98, p. 148). The thrust of the Housing Policy of the Government of India (GOI), thus, shifted from a short-term project-based approach to one of being considered as an integral component of economic development. The role of the GOI has accordingly changed from an agent that provided to that of a facilitator (GOI, 1994-95, p. 164).

1.4 National Agenda for Governance

The National Agenda for Governance (NAG) has identified housing for all as a priority area with particular emphasis on the needs of the vulnerable groups. Under the Special Action Plan, two million additional houses were targeted to be constructed every year. Out of this, 0.7 million houses were targeted to be constructed in urban areas and 1.3 million in rural areas (GOI, 2000-2001, p. 206).

1.5 National Housing Bank

The National Housing Bank (NHB) aims to enhance the flow of funds particularly in rural areas and its easy accessibility to the needy rural population. Till the end of April 1996, NHB subscribed to the "Special Rural Housing Debentures" (SRHDs) of State Level Cooperative Land Development Banks (SLDBs) to the tune of Rs. 180.91 crore (GOI, 1996-97, p. 193). In 1999-2000 Budget, the Government of India announced that the Golden Jubilee Rural Housing Finance Scheme of National Housing Bank would target 1.25 lakh dwelling units (GOI, 1999-2000, p. 178).

1.6 Housing Policies in India's Plans

Since the introduction of Minimum Needs Programme (MNP) in India's Five- Year Plans in the 1970s, housing came to be a component of MNP. Housing as a policy objective was there before 1970s also, but it remained as a welfare scheme separated from the broader dimensions that determine the quality of life of people. We briefly mention here how the problem of rural housing was looked into in the Plans adopted by Government of India from the beginning.

The subject of housing is not specifically mentioned in the seventh schedule of the Constitution of India which deals with matters coming within the purview of the Union and State Legislatures (GOI, Planning Commission, 1951-56, p. 598). The First Five-Year Plan (1951-56), however, suggested that the State Governments should concentrate on ameliorating conditions of housing in rural areas. The Plan opined that the pressure of population shifts towards cities, and the slum problems resulting therefrom, cannot be solved without ameliorating rural living conditions.

(a) Improvement in standards of rural housing in the First Plan aimed at :

- Utilizing labour and materials locally available including timber, bamboo, lime, clay, stone, gypsum, sand, kaolin, murram, jungle wood, grass and waste products of various types,
- Adequate water supply,
- Simple devices for ventilation,
- Provision of chimneys in the kitchen to draw away smoke,
- Use of erosion-resistant mud plaster for walls and roofs of improved materials and designs,
- Arrangements for disposal of sewage and waste products (GOI, Planning Commission, 1951-56, p. 606).

(b) Government Intervention in rural housing was planned :

- By demonstrating improved standards through model houses built in selected areas,
- By assisting the villager to build better types of houses within his means and with the resources readily available to him through methods of aided self-help,
- Introducing pilot schemes of model housing

> and better living conditions in selected rural areas (GOI, Planning Commission, 1951-56, pp. 598, 605).

During the First Plan, in community project areas, 58,000 rural latrines, 1600 miles of drains and 20,000 wells were constructed and 34,000 wells renovated; the corresponding figures in national extension areas were 80,000 rural latrines, 2700 miles of drains, 30,000 new wells and 51,000 renovated wells. In national extension and community project areas, about 29,000 houses were constructed and about the same number reconditioned (GOI, Planning Commission, 1956-61, p. 560).

The Second Plan (1956-61) looked at rural housing as a basic condition of rural reconstruction. The objectives of rural housing, thus, included rural water supply, drainage, sanitation, roads, welfare programmes for scheduled castes and other backward classes, programmes for providing more work and better living conditions for village artisans, proper spacing of houses, and the location of community buildings (GOI, Planning Commission, 1956-61, p. 559). The Second Plan stressed on Non-Government forces for construction of rural houses centered on utilization of bulk of materials locally available, voluntary cooperative labour, local community action, and self-help programmes (GOI, Planning Commission, 1956-61, p. 559). The Plan stressed on Government intervention for construction of rural houses through demonstrations of model houses and model villages, provision of improved designs and lay-outs, pilot experiments relating to the uses of local materials, organization of co-operative village programmes based on voluntary labour, financial assistance, especially for Harijans and other backward classes (GOI, Planning Commission, 1956-61, p. 560). During the Second Five-Year Plan, layout plans of 1600 villages were drawn up and loans amounting to Rs. 3.6 crores were sanctioned for construction of about 15,400 houses (GOI, Planning Commission, 1961-66, p. 694).

The Third Plan (1961-66) considered rural housing as an integral part of community development and village planning. The Plan pledged to 'link up the programme more closely with different schemes of community development such as provision of water supply, roads, drainage, public health, education' (GOI, Planning Commission, 1961-66, p. 696). The essential objective was to help create healthy environmental conditions for all sections of the village population and for balanced development of rural life as a whole. 'The specific programme for rural housing as such is intended to supplement the resources of the community development movement at the level of the block and the village by way of assistance of a number of types.' (GOI, Planning Commission, 1961-66, p. 694) This includes technical advice, demonstration, provision of improved designs and layouts, better use of local materials, and, to a limited extent, provisions of finance. The Third Plan pledged assistance in the shape of loans up to 66.6 per cent of the cost of construction, subject to a maximum of Rs. 2,000 per house, acquisition of land required for streets, community buildings, new house sites, and thinning out densities. The Plan suggested that priority in use of resources should be for the extension of the village site. The Plan also talked about improvement of roads and drainage, allotment of land to the community as a whole, use of local materials, economy of construction cost, cultural traditions and background of the locality and functional requirements of rural life (GOI, Planning Commission, 1961-66, p. 695).

The objectives of the Fourth Plan (1969-74) for rural housing were to get appropriate layouts made for the growing villages, to provide basic amenities such as water and sanitation facilities, to stimulate private building and renewal activity. The strategy for execution of the policy relied on co-operative effort, special housing schemes in favour of Scheduled Castes and other disadvantageously placed classes, laws conferring property rights for Scheduled Castes and land vested in the State to be utilized to provide house sites (Planning Commission, 1969-74, pp. 403-404).

The policy objectives of the Fifth Plan (1974-79) for rural housing were providing basic infrastructure and encouraging private initiative so that the people can construct the bulk of the housing, large scale provision of house sites for landless labourers in rural areas (GOI, Planning Commission, 1983, pp.6).

Rural housing did not receive much attention during the first 25 years of planning. The rehabilitation programmes of the Ministry of Refugees Rehabilitation provided, until around 1960, housing to about 5 lakh households, mainly in Northern India. A Village Housing Scheme was also launched in 1957 as part of the community development movement. Under this scheme, loans were provided to individuals and co-operatives, subject to a ceiling of Rs. 5,000 per house. 67,000 houses were built under this scheme by the end of the Fifth Plan (GOI, Planning Commission, 1992-97, p. 281).

The policy objectives for rural housing in the Sixth Plan (1980-85) were to provide house sites and assistance for housing rural landless labourers, to provide social housing schemes to cater to economically weaker sections (GOI, Planning Commission, 1983, p. 5). The policy objectives for rural housing in the Sixth Plan were to ensure housing requirements of rural landless labourers to be linked with the Minimum Needs Programme (MNP). development of residential plots, approach roads and tubewell for each cluster of 30 to 40 families (GOI, Planning Commission, Sixth Five-Year Plan, p. 391).

Of the 7.7 million landless families who have been allotted house sites by March 1985, only 0.56 million families have been given construction assistance. The Sixth Plan made provision for Rs. 250 per family for developed plots, approach roads and a masonry tube-well for each cluster of 30 to 40 families. The Plan envisaged construction assistance of Rs. 500 per family. This assumes that the beneficiaries will supply all labour inputs. A major initiative was taken in the Sixth Plan (1980-85), when the public sector was entrusted with a promotional role in housing in general and restricting its direct operations to housing for the urban poor. It also ensured provision of house sites and construction assistance for rural landless labourers (GOI, 1997-2002, p. 279).

In order to ensure the operation of the schemes more realistic, the Seventh Plan (1985-90) proposed to provide assistance to the extent of Rs. 500 per family for provision of developed house sites of 90 sq. metre each and assistance of Rs. 2,000 per family towards construction cost. All labour inputs were supposed to be provided by the beneficiary. During the Seventh Plan, the funds for rural housing from public institutions (HUDCO and GIC) were around Rs. 240 crores (GOI, Planning Commission, 1985-90, pp. 294-295).

The scheme of allotment of house sites and construction assistance to rural landless workers and artisans including SCs and STs was initiated in 1971 as a Central Sector scheme which was later transferred to State sector in 1974. This scheme is a part of the Minimum Needs Programme. Under the MNP, higher priority was accorded to this scheme during the Seventh Plan, setting apart a sum of Rs. 576.9 crores. As many as 43.2 lakhs house sites, as against the target of 29 lakhs, were allotted and construction assistance provided to 22.5 lakhs families (GOI, Planning Commission, 1992-97, p. 364).

The Eighth Plan (1992-97) accepted housing as a priority area, in the sense of being a basic need and a labour-intensive activity, the latter offering non-concentrated employment opportunities. The strategy aims at building an environment that provides assistance to the disadvantaged social groups including rural and urban poor, scheduled castes and scheduled tribes, physically handicapped, widows, and single woman (GOI, 1993-94, p. 155; GOI, 1996, Sept., p. 114). Public housing thrust, thus, is directed towards social housing to reach out housing solutions to priority groups. During the Eighth Plan period, major activities were initiated towards the implementation of Agenda-21, endorsed at the Rio de Janeiro Environment Meeting of 1992. The Agenda-21 stressed on the deteriorating situation in conditions of human settlement. The Government of India responded by adopting the National Housing Policy (NHP) 1994. The Ninth Plan accepted the fact that there was an enormous shortage in the housing sector and major deficiencies in the housing related infrastructure (GOI, Planning Commission, 1992-97, p. 282). Several programmes were initiated, such as the establishment of a housing finance system with a National Housing Bank at the apex level to overcome the problem.

While acknowledging the necessity of housing for all, the Ninth Plan (1997-2002) identified the priority groups of households for such support, such as people below poverty line, SC/ST, disabled, freed bonded labourers, slum dwellers and women headed households (GOI, Planning Commission, 1992-97, p. 283).

The magnitude of the housing problem grew since 1991 as documented in the Census. The 1991 Census put rural housing shortage at 137.20 lakh, of which 34.10 lakh households were without shelter and 103.10 lakh households lived in '*kutcha* unserviceable houses'.

During the Tenth Plan (2002-2007), free houses under Indira Awaas Yojana were planned to be provided largely to SC/ST, BPL families. For other BPL families, there would be a gradual shift to a credit-linked housing programme (Planning Commission, GOI, Tenth Five-Year Plan, Vol. II, p. 307). As observed by the Tenth Planning Commission, the provision of free houses meant that other loan-based schemes did not take off. This included the failure of credit-cum-subsidy scheme for rural housing introduced in 1999-2000 (Planning Commission, GOI, Tenth Five-Year Plan, Vol. II, pp. 299, 307).

Rural Housing in the Eleventh Five Year Plan (2007-2012)

The Eleventh Plan tells that 'the role of the State Government is confined to mere facilitating use of local, low cost, environment-friendly, and disaster-resistant technology and also in encouraging construction of sanitary latrine and smokeless *chulha*. ...The beneficiaries construct the houses as per their own choice of design, technology, and requirement' (Planning Commission, 2008, Vol. III, p. 94). The Eleventh Planning Commission opined that the Indira Awaas Yojana succeeded in empowering the poorest.

1.7 Housing Condition in India and Uttarakhand

Food, clothing, and shelter come first among all basic needs of people. Housing comes under private shelter. The Census of India provides detailed information about the housing condition of India and the state of UP. The National Sample Survey Organization (NSSO) Report, 1999 also provides information regarding housing condition in India and U.P.

1.7.1 Census 2001 : A Review on Housing

In rural Uttarakhand, total occupied houses as percentage of total number of houses, following Census 2001, stood at 91.1, the rest of the houses remaining vacant. The corresponding percentage of occupied houses at the all-India level was 94.7. Of the total number of houses, residence by use in rural Uttarakhand was 55.9 per cent, which was much less than the all-India rural percentage at 72.7. Houses for purposes other than residence in rural Uttarakhand were 25.4 per cent of total number of houses that was much less than that for rural India (12.8 per cent). Houses for purposes other than residence in rural Uttarakhand were very rare that covered houses for shops and office, educational and health institutions, factories and places of worship. The same was true for rural India (Table 1.1).

Table 1.1: Census Houses and Distribution Based on Types of Uses : Uttarakhand and India

Types of Houses	*Uttarakhand*		*India*	
	Rural	*Total*	*Rural*	*Total*
Residence	55.9	58.1	72.7	72.0
Residence cum-other Uses	2.8	2.9	3.4	3.2
Shop/Office	3.8	6.1	3.1	5.4
School/College	1.0	0.9	0.7	0.6
Hotel/Lodge/Guest House	0.2	0.3	0.2	0.2
Hospital/ Dispensary	0.2	0.3	0.2	0.2
Factory/ Workshop	0.5	0.6	0.6	0.9
Place of Worship	1.2	1.0	1.1	1.0
Other Non-Residence	25.4	21.1	12.8	10.2
Total Occupied Houses	91.1	91.3	94.7	93.7
Vacant Houses	8.9	8.7	5.3	6.3
Total No. of Houses	2012630 (100.0)	2566282 (100.0)	177537513 (100.0)	249095869 (100.0)

Source : Census of India, 2001.

Following Census 2001, two-thirds of all households in Uttarakhand lived in good houses, while 30.5 per cent lived in livable houses and 3.5 per cent in dilapidated conditions. The corresponding figures for all-India were projected as half of all houses as good, 44.1 as livable and 5.6 as dilapidated. The corresponding percentage for households in rural Uttarakhand were 64.4 as good, 32.1 as livable and 3.6 as dilapidated while the percentage for rural India were 45.0, 48.7 and 6.3 respectively. The households living in good houses in Uttarakhand, both total and rural, were better off relative to all-India distribution of households living in such houses (Table 1.2).

Table 1.2 : Distribution of Households by the Condition of Houses Occupied by them : Uttarakhand and India

Types of Houses	*Condition of Houses*	*Uttarakhand*		*India*	
		Rural	*Total*	*Rural*	*Total*
Residence	Good	64.4	66.0	45.0	50.4
	Livable	32.1	30.5	48.7	44.1
	Dilapidated	3.6	3.5	6.3	5.6
	Total	100.0	100.0	100.0	100.0
Residence-cum-other Uses	Good	62.5	64.5	42.0	46.7
	Livable	34.7	32.9	53.4	49.1
	Dilapidated	2.9	2.6	4.6	4.2
	Total	100.0	100.0	100.0	100.0
Total	Good	64.3	65.9	44.8	50.2
	Livable	32.2	30.6	48.9	44.3
	Dilapidated	3.5	3.5	6.2	5.5
	Total	1196157 (100.0)	1586321 (100.0)	138271559 (100.0)	191963935 (100.0)

Source : Census of India, 2001.

Following Census 2001, the major materials used for construction of roof in rural Uttarakhand were slate (21.0 per cent of households), concrete (24.6 per cent of households), stone (21.0 per cent of households), bricks (15.0 per cent), grass, thatch, bamboo, and wood and mud taken together (10.3 per cent). The other materials used for roof include tiles (khaprail), plastic/polythene, asbestos sheet, etc. This contradicts sharply with the materials used for construction of roof in rural India where tiles (*khaprail*) is in major use (37.6 per cent), followed by grass, wood, thatch, bamboo and mud (27.7 per cent). The use of slate is 1.1 per cent, bricks (5.6 per cent), stone (6.3 per cent) and concrete (11.0 per cent). By classification of households by social categories like SCs and STs, the uses of materials for construction of roof that for all categories of households in rural Uttarakhand. A similar pattern was for SC households at the all-India level so far as uses of materials for construction of roof was concerned (Table 1.3).

Table 1.3: Distribution of Households Living in Houses by Materials of Roof : Uttarakhand and India

Types of Roof	*Uttarakhand*		*India*	
	Rural	*Total*	*Rural*	*Total*
Grass, Thatch, Bamboo, Wood, Mud	10.3	8.9	27.7	21.9
Plastic/Polythene	0.3	0.6	0.4	0.5
Tiles (*Khaprail*)	1.5	1.3	37.6	32.6
Slate	21.0	16.0	1.1	0.9
G.I. Metal/ Asbestos Sheet	5.9	8.0	9.8	11.6
Bricks	15.0	18.0	5.6	5.6
Stone	21.0	16.1	6.3	6.5
Concrete	24.6	30.7	11.0	19.8
Any other Material	0.3	0.4	0.6	0.6
Total	1196157 (100.0)	1586321 (100.0)	138271559 (100.0)	191963935 (100.0)

Note : The table excluded houses occupied by the institutional households for which data on condition of house were not collected.
Source : Census of India, 2001.

Following Census 2001, the major materials that were used for construction of walls in houses in rural Uttarakhand was stone (56.6 per cent) followed by bricks (30.1 per cent); tiles (*khaprail*) was used by 7.6 per cent of households in rural Uttarakhand; while grass, thatch, wood, bamboo and mud were used in case of 3.5 per cent households. The other uses were slate, asbestos sheet and concrete. In case of rural India, the major use for construction of houses was tiles (*khaprail*), followed by bricks (34.2 per cent), grass, thatch, bamboo, wood and mud (12.6 per cent) and stone (10.5 per cent). The use of stone in the hilly regions of rural Uttarakhand, thus, was much ahead of that of rural India in construction of walls in houses. The pattern of use of materials for walls by SCs in Uttarakhand was similar to that for all households in rural Uttarakhand. The same was true for SC households at the all-India level as far as use of materials for walls was concerned (Table 1.4).

Table 1.4 : Distribution of Households Living in Houses by Major Materials of Wall : Uttarakhand and India

Type of Wall	*Uttarakhand*		*India*	
	Rural	*Total*	*Rural*	*Total*
Grass, Thatch, Bamboo, Wood, Mud	3.5	3.1	12.6	10.2
Plastic/Polythene	0.1	0.1	0.3	0.3
Tiles (*Khaprail*)	7.6	6.9	39.7	32.2
Slate	1.0	0.9	0.9	0.9
G.I. Metal/ Asbestos Sheet	0.4	0.6	0.4	0.6
Bricks	30.1	43.0	34.2	43.7
Stone	56.6	44.3	10.5	9.4
Concrete	0.7	0.9	1.2	2.4
Any other Material	0.0	0.0	0.2	0.2
Total	1196157 (100.0)	1586321 (100.0)	138271559 (100.0)	191963935 (100.0)

Source : Census of India, 2001.

Following Census 2001, the main material in construction of floor in rural Uttarakhand was mud (68.2 per cent) followed by concrete (24.5 per cent). The same was true for SC households. The other materials that were in use were wood, bamboo, stone, and tiles. At the level of rural India, the main materials for construction of wall were mud (72.3 per cent) followed by cement (18.0 per cent). This was similar to the use of materials for SC households at the rural India level (Table 1.5).

Table 1.5 : Distribution of Households Living in Houses by Major Materials of Floor: Uttarakhand and India

Types of Floor	*Uttarakhand*		*India*	
	Rural	*Total*	*Rural*	*Total*
Mud	68.2	55.1	72.3	57.1
Wood, Bamboo	2.9	2.3	0.8	0.7
Bricks	0.9	1.2	2.0	2.3
Stone	2.5	2.1	4.5	5.8
Cement	24.5	35.9	18.0	26.5
Mosaic, Floor Tiles	0.9	3.4	2.2	7.3
Any Other Material	0.1	0.1	0.2	0.4
Total	1196157 (100.0)	1586321 (100.0)	138271559 (100.0)	191963935 (100.0)

Source : Census of India, 2001.

Of all the houses following Census 2001, 85.1 per cent was permanent in rural Uttarakhand which was only 41.1 per cent in rural India. Semi-permanent houses by characteristics of construction were 35.7 per cent at rural India level that was only 6.9 per cent at rural Uttarakhand level. Among temporary houses, there were two categories, one serviceable and the other non-serviceable. Non-serviceable was 8.4 per cent in case of rural India that was 3.1 per cent in case of rural Uttarakhand. Temporary houses in rural India were 23.1 per cent for rural India that was only 8.0 per cent in case of rural Uttarakhand. By social categories of households, the houses by durability/types for SCs in Uttarakhand was similar to that in rural Uttarakhand, and for SCs in India was similar to that in rural India (Table 1.6).

Table 1.6 : Distribution of Households by Types of Houses Occupied : Uttarakhand and India

Types of Houses	*Uttarakhand*		*India*	
	Rural	*Total*	*Rural*	*Total*
Permanent	85.1	86.3	41.1	51.8
Semi-Permanent	6.9	6.6	35.7	30.0
Temporary Serviceable	4.9	4.3	14.7	11.5
Temporary Non-serviceable	3.1	2.8	8.4	6.6
Temporary Total	8.0	7.1	23.1	18.1
Unclassifiable	0.0	0.0	0.0	0.0
Total	1196157 (100.0)	1586321 (100.0)	138271559 (100.0)	191963935 (100.0)

Source : Census of India, 2001.

In rural Uttarakhand, most of the households (33.0 per cent) had members between six and eight, followed by 18.7 per cent of households constituted by five members, and 15.1 per cent of households constituted by four members. One member household was only 6.1 per cent. A similar pattern of households by size was true for Uttarakhand as a whole and SC households in Uttarakhand. In case of rural India, households by size between six and eight members were 29.6

per cent and reflected similar pattern for rural Uttarakhand. Large size households, thus, were more common for households in case of rural Uttarakhand, rural India and by social categories by SC households.

Following Census 2001, most of the households in rural Uttarakhand had two dwelling rooms in their residential houses (32.7 per cent of the households), followed by one-room house (24.9 per cent), four rooms (16.6 per cent) and three rooms (13.6 per cent). The same pattern by distribution of households by number of dwelling rooms was true for all Uttarakhand. For rural India most of the households had one room house (39.8 per cent) followed by two rooms (30.2 per cent), three rooms (13.3 per cent) and four rooms (7.0 per cent). Thus, houses in rural regions of both India and Uttarakhand, mostly have one or two rooms. For SC households in particular, 72.3 per cent of the households in rural Uttarakhand had one or two rooms which was 77.7 per cent for all-India. It is also reported in the census data that 3.4 per cent of the houses in rural India had no exclusive room which was true for 1.0 per cent of households in rural Uttarakhand.

Following Census 2001, 90.5 per cent of the houses in rural Uttarakhand were owned by the households, which was 94.4 per cent for rural India. The houses rented in rural Uttarakhand were 5.4 per cent of households, which was 3.6 per cent for rural India.

The major sources of drinking water for both Uttarakhand and India, following Census 2001, were tap, hand-pump, tube-well, well, tank-pond-lake, river-canal-spring and other such sources. Tap was generally located within the premise of the residential house, and often within a distance of 500 metres, for both Uttarakhand and India. So was for rural Uttarakhand. However, for rural India, location of tap was often outside the premise as reported by the households. For Uttarakhand and rural Uttarakhand, tap was the major source of drinking water followed by hand-pump, as reported by the households. The other sources of water were not of much importance for drinking purposes. The same was true for all-India and rural India.

For one (married) couple in the houses of rural Uttarakhand, 74.2 per cent of the households reported to have one room at least. For two couples living in a house, 12.3 per cent of the households reported to have two rooms and 20.9 per cent reported to have three rooms and above in rural Uttarakhand. This was reported by 15.3 per cent of the households in rural India. In case of rural India, one couple living in a house got one room as reported by 79.0 per cent of the households. The matching of number of rooms in a house for rural India and rural Uttarakhand was clear for a single couple living in a house relative to the mismatch for couple more than one and number of rooms in a house.

In rural Uttarakhand, 73.7 per cent of the married couples had independent sleeping room which was only 58.6 per cent in case of rural India. There was thus large gap between requirement of independent sleeping room and number of couples in both rural Uttarakhand and rural India, more so in case of rural India.

Following Census 2001, percentage of households having bathroom available in houses in rural Uttarakhand (26.0 per cent) was much ahead of that of rural India (22.8 per cent). However, these percentages were similar for all Uttarakhand and all-India (respectively 38.8 and 36.1 per cent). For rural Uttarakhand, no latrine was a phenomenon for 63.6 per cent of the households/houses had no latrine, which rural India. For all-India absence of latrine in houses (63.6 per cent) was much more than that of all-Uttarakhand (54.3 per cent). Absence of any drainage was a major phenomenon in rural Uttarakhand (65.0 per cent households reporting), which was 65.8 per cent for rural India. For all-Uttarakhand and all-India drainage by absence was similar.

The major sources of lighting at night in rural

Uttarakhand were electricity and kerosene similar to that in rural India. This remains true for all Uttarakhand and all-India. The other sources like solar energy, other types of oil were marginally used (Table 1.7).

Table 1.7 : Distribution of Households by Sources of Lighting : Uttarakhand and India

Sources of Lighting	*Uttarakhand*		*India*	
	Rural	*Total*	*Rural*	*Total*
Electricity	50.3	60.3	43.5	55.8
Kerosene	46.7	37.3	55.6	43.3
Solar Energy	2.4	1.9	0.3	0.3
Other Oil	0.1	0.1	0.1	0.1
Any Other	0.2	0.2	0.2	0.2
No Lighting	0.3	0.3	0.3	0.3
Total	1196157 (100.0)	1586321 (100.0)	138271559 (100.0)	191963935 (100.0)

Source : Census of India, 2001.

In rural Uttarakhand, 68.3 per cent of the households had separate kitchen, which was for 71.3 per cent of all households in Uttarakhand. The corresponding percentages for rural India and all-India were 59.4 and 64.0. The types of fuel used for cooking were firewood, crop residue, LPG, electricity, bio-gas, cowdung cake, and kerosene. Firewood was the major source of fuel for cooking in rural Uttarakhand (67.5 per cent of households reporting), followed by use of LPG (21.3 per cent). The uses of other types of fuel were much less for the households. In rural India, the major fuel was firewood (64.1 per cent reporting), followed by crop residue (13.1 per cent) and cowdung cake (12.8 per cent). Use of LPG was much less (5.7 per cent) at the rural India level. Overall, for all-Uttarakhand and all-India, it was firewood (52.5 per cent for India and 54.6 per cent for Uttarakhand) that came first in ranking of fuel for cooking followed by LPG (respectively 18.5 and 33.5 per cent). At the level of all Uttarakhand, uses of crop residue and cow-dung were much less relative to all-India level.

The distribution of households by ownership over white goods by Census data 2001 shows that only 6.2 per cent of the households in rural Uttarakhand had scooter, motor cycle or moped while as high as 42.8 per cent in rural India owned them. Ownership of television was much higher for rural Uttarakhand (32.3 per cent) relative to rural India (18.9 per cent); also ownership of radio/transistor in rural Uttarakhand (51.4 per cent) was higher than that of rural India (31.5 per cent). Bicycle was owned by more households in rural India (42.8 per cent) relative to that in rural Uttarakhand (25.9 per cent). Ownership of telephone was marginal for rural Uttarakhand (4.4 per cent) and rural India (3.8 per cent). The ownership over other assets like car, jeep and van was insignificant in both rural Uttarakhand and rural India (Table 1.8).

Table 1.8 : Number of Households having each of the Specified Assets : Uttarakhand and India

Households Having	*Uttarakhand*		*India*	
	Rural	*Total*	*Rural*	*Total*
Radio-Transistor	51.4	49.7	31.5	35.1
Television	32.3	42.9	18.9	31.6
Telephone	4.4	9.9	3.8	9.1
Bicycle	25.9	30.9	42.8	43.7
Scooter, Motor Cycle & Moped	6.2	11.9	42.8	43.7
Car, Jeep & Van	1.3	2.7	1.3	2.5
None of specified	30.1	25.7	40.5	34.5
Total Households	1196157 (100.0)	1586321 (100.0)	138271559 (100.0)	191963935 (100.0)

Source : Census of India, 2001.

1.7.2 A Review on Housing based on National Sample Survey, 2004

Following NSS 58th Round, the households having sources of drinking water within dwelling premise in rural

Uttarakhand (34.4 per cent) was much ahead of that of rural India (18.0 per cent). The source outside the dwelling but within premises was much more in case of rural India (19.2 per cent) relative to rural Uttarakhand (11.3 per cent). Most of the households (around two-thirds in each case) in rural India and rural Uttarakhand had sources of drinking water outside (Table 1.9).

Table 1.9 : Rural Households by Distance to the Sources of Drinking Water

Distance		*Uttarakhand*	*India*
Within Dwelling		34.4	18.0
Outside dwelling but within premises		11.3	19.2
Outside premises at a distance of	Less than 0.2 km.	47.0	50.9
	0.2 to 0.5 km.	5.1	9.0
	0.5 to 1.0 km.	1.1	1.8
	1.0 to 1.6 km.	0.8	0.4
	1.6 km. or more	0.0	0.3
NR		0.4	0.4
Total		1191388 (100.0)	148051155 (100.0)

Note : The estimated households are basis of proportion value given in the data and estimated number of households.

Source : Housing Condition in India, Housing Stock and Constructions, NSS 58th Round, Report No. 488, 2004.

While in case of all-India, 76.0 per cent of the households did not have bathroom in their houses, it was 62.6 per cent in case of Uttarakhand. 14.3 per cent of the households in Uttarakhand had attached bathroom that was 9.8 per cent in case of India.

While 76.3 per cent of the households in India did not have latrines, 61.2 per cent of the households in Uttarakhand did not have the same. 8.7 per cent of the households in India, and 25.0 per cent in Uttarakhand had own latrines. The rest were shared latrines and public (community) latrines (Table 1.10).

Table 1.10 : Rural Households by Types of Latrine

Types of Latrine		*Uttarakhand*	*India*
Own	Septic tank/flush	25.0	8.7
	Pit	4.7	7.5
	Service	0.4	1.1
Shared	Septic tank/flush	3.7	1.9
	Pit	0.6	0.6
	Service	0.2	0.2
Public	Septic tank/flush	2.2	1.1
Community	Pit	0.4	0.3
	Service	0.0	0.6
Other		1.6	1.6
No Latrine		61.2	76.3
	Total	1191388 (100.0)	148051155 (100.0)

Note : The estimated households are basis of proportion value given in the data and estimated number of households.

Source : Housing Condition in India, Housing Stock and Constructions, NSS 58th Round, Report No. 488, 2004.

For rural households in both Uttarakhand and India, the plinth area in houses for living varied between 20 and 100 sq.mt. For Uttarakhand, the percentage of such households was 88.0 while for India it was 79.9. Less than one per cent of the households in Uttarakhand had plinth area in houses more than 200 metres which was true for 1.9 per cent in India.

By uses of houses, households in rural Uttarakhand using houses for residential purposes only was 98.4 per cent that was 95.1 per cent for rural India. The other purposes for use of houses like factory, office, shop were negligible (Table 1.11).

70.8 per cent of the rural households reported to have *pucca* houses that were 35.9 per cent for rural houses in India. In case of rural households in Uttarakhand, unserviceable *katcha* houses were negligible (0.8 per cent) that was 6.4 per cent for India. Semi-*pucca* houses for rural households in Uttarakhand were 22.4 per cent which was reported by 42.8 per cent in India. Serviceable *katcha* houses were reported by rural households (14.9 per cent) in India that was 6.1 per cent for Uttarakhand (Table 1.12).

Table 1.11: Rural Households by Types of Use of Houses

Types of Use of houses	*Uttarakhand*	*India*
Residential only	98.4	95.1
Residential-cum-factory	0.4	0.6
Residential-cum-office	0.0	0.2
Residential-cum-shop	0.6	1.7
Residential cum factory/office/shop	0.6	0.3
Others	0.0	2.1
Total	1191388 (100.0)	148051155 (100.0)

Note : The estimated households are basis of proportion value given in the data and estimated number of households.

Source : Housing Condition in India, Housing Stock and Constructions, NSS 58th Round, Report No. 488, 2004.

Table 1.12 : Rural Households by Status of Houses

Status of Houses	*Uttarakhand*	*India*
Pucca	70.8	35.9
Semi-*Pucca*	22.4	42.8
Serviceable *Katcha*	6.1	14.9
Unservicable *Katcha*	0.8	6.4
No response	0.0	0.1
Total	1191388 (100.0)	148051155 (100.0)

Note : The estimated households are basis of proportion value given in the data and estimated number of households.

Source : Housing Condition in India, Housing Stock and Constructions, NSS 58th Round, Report No. 488, 2004.

By durability, the rural houses in Uttarakhand as well as in India varied over a wide range of years and hence, the condition of the structure of the houses showed differential. However, the good or bad quality of the house was not necessarily in proportion to the house by years constructed. For example, the rural houses built around ten years ago were thought to be in good condition for 14.8 per cent of houses while for the houses built between 10 years and 20 years ago the good condition was for 17.1 per cent of the houses. For houses built 40 to 60 years ago, the good condition held good for 2.2 per cent of the houses. For rural houses in India, while 12.0 per cent reported were good which were built 10 years ago, 8.7 per cent were good which were built 10 to 20 years ago and 4.6 per cent good which were built 20 to 40 years ago. Thus, we did not find any direct or inverse relation between age of house and quality of house in each of rural Uttarakhand and rural India.

Following NSS 58th Round, 52.3 per cent of the rural households had no drainage which was for 61.8 per cent of households in India. Open *katcha* drain was reported by 20.1 per cent households in rural Uttarakhand which was for 20.4 per cent in rural India. Covered *pucca* drain was for 7.1 per cent of the households in rural Uttarakhand, which was for 2.9 per cent in rural India (Table 1.13).

Table 1.13 : Rural Households by Types of Drainage in the Houses

Type of Drainages	*Uttarakhand*	*India*
Underground	2.5	2.0
Covered *Pucca*	7.1	2.9
Open *Pucca*	17.8	13.0
Open *Katcha*	20.1	20.4
No Drainage	52.3	61.8
No response	0.1	0.0
Total	1191388 (100.0)	148051155 (100.0)

Note : The estimated households are basis of proportion value given in the data and estimated number of households.

Source : Housing Condition in India, Housing Stock and Constructions, NSS 58th Round, Report No. 488, 2004.

The major materials for construction of floor for rural houses in Uttarakhand were mud (48.3 per cent) that was 64.1 per cent for India. The next material in ranking was cement, for 34.6 per cent in houses in rural Uttarakhand and 24.0 per cent in rural India. The other materials for construction of floor were brick, and stone that came third in ranking for each, and then wood, bamboo, and mosaic tiles (Table 1.14).

Table 1.14 : Rural Households by Types of Floor of the Dwelling Units

Types of Floor	*Uttarakhand*	*India*
Mud	48.3	64.1
Bamboo/log	0.3	0.4
Wood/Plank	2.7	0.4
Brick/Lime Stone/Stone	12.6	8.1
Cement	34.6	24.0
Mosaic tiles	1.5	2.8
Other Types	0.0	0.2
No response	0.0	0.0
Total Number	1191388 (100.0)	148051155 (100.0)

Note : The estimated households are basis of proportion value given in the data and estimated number of households.

Source : Housing Condition in India, Housing Stock and Constructions, NSS 58th Round, Report No. 488, 2004.

For rural Uttarakhand, the major material for building wall in residential houses was burnt brick/stone (65.4 per cent) followed by cement/RBC/RCC (24.7 per cent) and mud (8.8 per cent). For rural India, the wall constructed by burnt brick/stone was for 47.5 per cent, followed by mud (36.7 per cent) and grass/straw/leaves/bamboo 9.8 per cent (Table 1.15).

Table 1.15 : Rural Households by Types of Wall of Dwelling Unit

Wall's Materials	*Uttarakhand*	*India*
Grass/Straw/Leaves/Reed/Bamboo	0.9	9.8
Mud (with /without bamboo)/ Unburnt Brick	8.8	36.3
Canvass/Cloth	0.0	0.1
Other *Katcha* Materials	0.0	1.1
Timber	0.2	0.4
Burnt Brick/Stone/Lime Stone	65.4	47.5
Iron or Other Metal sheet	0.0	0.2
Cement/RBC/RCC	24.7	4.5
Other *Pucca* Materials	0.0	0.2
Total	1191388 (100.0)	148051155 (100.0)

Note : The estimated households are basis of proportion value given in the data and estimated number of households.

Source : Housing Condition in India, Housing Stock and Constructions, NSS 58th Round, Report No. 488, 2004.

Following NSS 58th Round, the major material for construction of roof in dwelling unit in rural Uttarakhand was cement/RBC/RCC followed by burnt brick/stone, tiles/slate, and grass/straw/leaves/bamboo. In rural India, the major material for building of roof was tiles/slate followed by grass/straw/leaves/bamboo, cement/RBC/RCC, burnt brick/stone, iron/zinc/asbestos (Table 1.16).

Table 1.16 : Rural Households by Types of Roof of Dwelling Units

Types of Roof	*Uttarakhand*	*India*
Grass/Straw/Leaves/Reed/Bamboo	6.5	20.1
Mud /Unburnt Brick	1.9	3.5
Canvass/Cloth	0.1	0.2
Other *Katcha* Materials	0.1	1.7
Tiles/Slate	18.1	31.1
Burnt Brick/Stone/Lime Stone	19.2	13.2
Iron/Zinc/ Other Metal sheet/ Asbestos sheet	5.2	10.4
Cement/RBC/RCC	45.6	17.7
Other *Pucca* Materials	3.2	2.0
Total	1191388 (100.0)	148051155 (100.0)

Note : The estimated households are basis of proportion value given in the data and estimated number of households.

Source : Housing Condition in India, Housing Stock and Constructions, NSS 58th Round, Report No. 488, 2004.

Most of the rural households in Uttarakhand (75.0 per cent) have per capita floor space between 10 and 75 sq. mt. that was true for 77.4 per cent of the rural households in India. Per capita floor area less than 10 sq. mt. was rare for each of rural Uttarakhand and rural India. 17.2 per cent of the households in rural Uttarakhand had per capita floor area more than 100 sq. mt. that was for 16.2 per cent in rural India (Table 1.17).

The average cost of construction per square metre in rural Uttarakhand for new building was Rs. 2,553.00 and for rural India Rs. 1,851.00. For rural Uttarakhand before March 1999, the average cost was higher than the overall average

Table 1.17: Rural Households by Per Capita Floor Area of the Dwelling Unit

Per Capita Floor area (in sq.m)	*Uttarakhand*	*India*
Less than 10	0.3	0.2
10 to 20	12.9	12.1
20 to 30	20.5	22.5
30 to 40	17.5	19.9
40 to 50	14.1	13.5
50 to 75	10.0	9.4
75 to 100	7.4	6.2
100 to 150	6.5	4.4
150 to 200	4.6	5.6
More than 200	6.1	6.2
Total	1191388 (100.0)	148051155 (100.0)

Note : The estimated households are basis of proportion value given in the data and estimated number of households.

Source : Housing Condition in India, Housing Stock and Constructions, NSS 58th Round, Report No. 488, 2004.

(covering all accounting periods) and again higher after April 2002. Between April 1999 and March 2002, the average cost of construction was lower than overall average. For rural India, the average cost was lower during April 2000 to March 2001 than the overall average and again after April 2002; for other periods, the average cost was higher for rural India relative to overall average (Table 1.18).

Table 1.18 : Average Cost of Construction per Square Metre in Rural Area for New Building

(in Rs.)

Duration	*Uttarakhand*	*India*
Within March 1999	2979	1899
April 1999 to March 2000	1772	1853
April 2000 to March 2001	2171	1695
April 2001 to March 2002	2525	1995
April 2002 or After	3150	1805
No response	0	2158
Total	2553	1851

Note : The estimated households are basis of proportion value given in the data and estimated number of households.

Source : Housing Condition in India, Housing Stock and Constructions, NSS 58th Round, Report No. 488, 2004.

The own sources satisfied 84.2 per cent of finance required for construction of house in Uttarakhand, followed by support from financial institutes (6.3 per cent), friends and relatives (5.4 per cent). The role of money lender was insignificant in Uttarakhand (1.9 per cent). Relative to this, in India, 66.2 per cent of finance was satisfied by own sources for construction of house, followed by money lenders (9.1 per cent), friends and relatives (8.9 per cent), financial institutes (6.5 per cent) (Table 1.19).

Table 1.19: Average Finance (Rs. in lakh) Collected for Construction of House by Sources of Finance

Sources of finance		*Uttarakhand*	*India*
Own sources		84.2	66.2
Cooperatives		0.8	3.2
Financial Institutes	Govt.	6.3	6.5
	Non-govt.	0.0	1.5
Non-Financial Institutes	Govt.	0.1	1.7
	Non-govt.	0.0	0.5
Money Lenders		1.9	9.1
Friends and Relatives		5.4	8.9
Others		1.4	2.3
Total		67468 (100.0)	33845 (100.0)

Note : The estimated households are based on proportion value given in the data and estimated number of households.

Source : Housing Condition in India, Housing Stock and Constructions, NSS 58th Round, Report No. 488, 2004.

In rural Uttarakhand, the material cost covered 72.1 per cent and labour 26.2 per cent while in rural India material cost covered 72.3 per cent and labour 20.8 per cent. Non-material non-labour cost was insignificant in Uttarakhand (1.7 per cent) and rural India (6.8 per cent) (Table 1.20).

1.8 Constraints in Execution of Government Schemes for Rural Housing

Under the existing system, the DRDAs/Zilla Parishads make

Table 1.20 : Average Cost Incurred in Rural Houses per Construction during Last One Year by type of Cost

Average Cost (Rs. per sq. meter)	*Uttarakhand*		*India*	
	No.	*%*	*No.*	*%*
Material *Pucca*	1056	54.2	700	60.2
Material Other	348	17.9	141	12.1
Labour	510	26.2	242	20.8
Other	34	1.7	79	6.8
Total	1948	100.0	1162	100.0

Note : The estimated households are basis of proportion value given in the data and estimated number of households.

Source : Housing Condition in India, Housing Stock and Constructions, NSS 58th Round, Report No. 488, 2004.

allocations and target how many houses are to be constructed for coverage of each Panchayat. Thereafter, the Gram Sabhas are expected to select the beneficiaries from the list of eligible households as per target for the Gram Panchayat. Given the huge size of potential beneficiaries waiting in queue for allotment of free houses, Gram Panchayats find it troublesome to select a few households each year. This could cause a conflict among the income poor households themselves. The pressure from the local MLAs and MPs may accentuate the problem (GOI, Planning Commission, 1997-2002, pp. 148-149).

The Government of India (GOI) did not pay much attention to housing as an imminent problem immediately after independence in 1947. The Ministry of Refugee Rehabilitation launched a housing programme for the rehabilitation of the refugees following partition of British India on both sides of the map, the east and the west. The programme lasted up to 1960. The Community Development Movement of 1957 saw the launching of a village housing scheme as its integral part. All these programmes were half-hearted. The Estimates Committee of the Lok Sabha pointed out in 1972-73 in its 37th Report that 'although 83 per cent of

India's population live in villages and about 73 per cent of the rural population reside in unsatisfactory *kutcha* structures, the problem of rural housing has not received the close attention of the Government'.

1.8.1 Indira Awaas Yojana (IAY)

The history of the Central Government initiated Indira Awaas Yojana (IAY) in 1980 can be traced to the programmes of rural employment. Construction of houses was one of the major activities under the National Rural Employment Programme (NREP), which began in 1980 and the Rural Landless Employment Guarantee Programme (RLEGP) which began in 1983. In 1985, the GOI announced to earmark a part of RLEGP fund for the construction of houses for SCs/STs and freed bonded labourers. The IAY, thus, was launched as a sub-scheme of RLEGP in 1985-86. Since the launching of Jawahar Rozgar Yojana (JRY) in April, 1989, Indira Awaas Yojana became a sub-scheme of JRY. Since January 1, 1996, IAY has been delinked from JRY. IAY since then became an independent scheme. This is a major scheme for construction of houses to be given to the poor, free of cost (GOI, 2001-2002, p. 244).

As a physical dwelling space, the IAY houses are supposed to be built on individual plots in the main habitation of the village. This is supposed to ensure safety and security of the household, proximity to workplace, and social accommodation (GOI, 1998, pp. 1, 3). 'The objective of the Indira Awaas Yojana is to provide dwelling units to the members of SC/ST and free bonded labour below the poverty line free of cost. The scheme has been extended to non-SC/ST rural poor subject to the condition that the benefits to non-SC/ST should not exceed 40 per cent of the total allocations. The permissible assistance per house is Rs. 20,000 in plain areas and Rs. 22,000 in hilly or difficult areas' (GOI, 1997-98, p. 148).

IAY addresses the problems of shelter faced by BPL families only. However, there are several other households just above the poverty line who belong to the Economically Weaker Sections (EWSs) and are in need of houses. There is virtually no institutional finance in the rural housing sector except for limited amounts provided by Housing and Urban Development Corporation (HUDCO) schemes (GOI, Planning Commission, 1997-2002, Mid-Term Appraisal, p. 148).

The ceiling on construction assistance under IAY at present is Rs. 25,000 per unit for plain areas and Rs. 27,500 for hilly / difficult areas. The ceiling for upgradation of house (from *kutcha* to semi-*pucca* or *pucca*) is presently Rs. 12,500. The construction of the residential unit is the responsibility of the assistance receiver, that is, the beneficiary. The Gram Sabha is supposed to select the beneficiaries through open meetings. The allotment of the house has to be in the name of the female member of the beneficiary household. The residential unit may also be allotted in the name of both husband and wife. The integral components of a residential unit under IAY are sanitary latrine and smokeless *chulhas*.. The houses under IAY are not to be built by any external agency like government departments, contractors, and NGOs.

1.8.1.1 Target Group

The target group for houses under IAY will be people below poverty line living in rural areas belonging to Scheduled Castes/Scheduled Tribes, freed bonded labourers and non-SC/ST subject to the condition that the benefits to non-SC/ST should not exceed 40 per cent of total IAY allocation during a financial year. From 1995-96, the IAY benefits have been extended to ex-servicemen, widows or next-of-kin of defence personnel and paramilitary forces killed in action irrespective of the income criteria subject to the condition that (i) they reside in rural areas; (ii) they have not been covered under any other scheme of shelter/rehabilitation; and (iii) they are houseless or in need of shelter or shelter upgradation. Priority is planned to be given to other ex-servicemen and retired members of the paramilitary forces as long as they fulfil the normal eligibility conditions of the Indira Awaas Yojana and have not been covered under any other shelter rehabilitation scheme. The priority in the matter of allotment of houses to the ex-servicemen and paramilitary forces and their dependents will be out of 40 per cent of the houses set apart for allotment among the non-SC/ST categories of beneficiaries. Three per cent of the funds have been earmarked for the benefit of disabled persons below poverty line. This reservation of 3 per cent under Indira Awaas Yojana for disabled persons below the poverty line would be horizontal reservation i.e., disabled persons belonging to sections like SCs, STs and others would fall in their respective categories.

1.8.1.2 Identification of Beneficiaries

District Rural Development Authority (DRDAs)/Zilla Parishads, on the basis of allocations made and targets fixed, shall decide Panchayat-wise number of houses to be constructed under "Indira Awaas Yojana" during a particular financial year and intimate the same to the Gram Panchayat. Thereafter, the Gram Sabha will select the beneficiaries restricting its number to the target allotted, from the list of eligible households, according to "Indira Awaas Yojana" guidelines and as per priorities fixed. No approval of the Panchayat Samiti will be required. The Panchayat Samiti should, however, be sent a list of selected beneficiaries for their information. This amendment in the "Indira Awaas Yojana" guidelines shall come into force with effect from 1-4-1998.

1.8.2 Pradhan Mantri Gramodaya Yojana (Gramin Awaas)

PMGY was introduced in 2000-2001 with the objective of focusing on village level development in five critical areas, i.e., health, primary education, drinking water, housing, and rural roads, with the overall objective of improving the quality of life of people in the rural areas. As a component of PMGY, the Awaas Yojana is to be implemented on the pattern of Indira Awaas Yojana with the objective of sustainable habitat development at the village level and to meet the growing housing needs of the rural poor (GOI, 2001-2002, p. 243).

1.8.3 Credit-cum-Subsidy Scheme (CCSS)

A Credit-cum-Subsidy Scheme for rural housing has been launched from April 1999 which targeted a rural family having annual income up to Rs. 32,000. The subsidy portion is restricted to Rs. 10,000 and loan amount to Rs. 40,000 (GOI, 1999-2000, p. 176). The Scheme covers both BPL and APL families (GOI, 1999-2000, p. 176).

1.9 Housing and Institutions : Role of Panchayati Raj System

The Constitution (Article 243G) provides for "devolution", that is, the empowerment of Panchayati Raj Institutions (PRIs) to function as institutions of self-government for the twin purposes of (i) making plans for economic development and social justice for their respective areas, and ii) implementing programmes of economic development and social justice in their respective areas, for subjects devolved to the PRIs, including those listed in the Eleventh Schedule, and subject to such conditions as the State may, by law, specify. Therefore, the key objective is to ensure that Panchayati Raj Institutions (PRIs) function as institutions of self-government rather than as mere implementing agencies for other authorities in respect of such functions as may be devolved on them. In order to make Panchayati Raj Institutions effective, there is need for providing functional and financial autonomy. It is also essential to ensure transparency in their functioning. Here, Gram Sabha can play a vital role. It can ensure social audit and villagers can fix responsibility on Panchayat functionaries. If Gram Sabha is empowered, people will realize its importance and make it more effective (First Round Table of Ministers-in-charge of Panchayati Raj, Kolkata, 24-25 July, 2004).

Under the Panchayati Raj Act, the state government has unrestricted power to fragment areas or to change the demographic composition and character of Panchayats. MPs, MLAs and MLCs are members of middle and apex-level Panchayats. At the Gram Panchayat level, a two-thirds majority is required to carry a motion of no-confidence. At other levels, a simple majority is enough. This gives scope for malpractice and instability; especially since membership at Panchayats is small, and when the Gram Sabhas have no real power. The Gram Sabhas meet twice a year, but their recommendations are not binding on the Panchayats. Women do not have appropriate representation on all committees. Panchayats do not have full financial or administrative freedom. They do not have the authority to pass their own budgets, and government approval is required to borrow funds. They even have to depend on the government for their personnel. The government has the power to remove an elected functionary and dissolve a Panchayat without any independent inquiry. Panchayats are merely viewed as extended government offices at different levels.

After the 73rd Constitutional amendment, the Government of India has been strengthening the Panchayats in all states/UTs. The UP government has strengthened the

Panchayats by the UP Panchayati Raj Act, 1997. Through this Act, a new structure of three-tier Panchayati Raj has come into the state. The UP Government has created a new department named "Panchayat" and given power for actual implementation of the rural development programmes. Most of the programmes like IAY, PMGRY, SGRY, SGSRY, ICDS, NAP, Pension Schemes, Mid-Day Meal, and Scholarship for students are implemented by the PRIs at grassroot level. The major role of the PRIs are selection of beneficiary, monitoring of the programmes and giving feedback to Government for better formulation of programmes and also formulating Panchayats plan for development of village. The same was adopted by the newly constituted state of Uttarakhand.

2

Housing in India and the Purpose of the Book

2.1 Purpose of the Book

In this book we have examined the role of rural housing for decent standard of living of rural population. We have covered houses constructed under Government schemes particularly under IAY as well as houses privately constructed in rural areas. Houses under Government-sponsored schemes are analyzed in two categories, namely, houses for the BPL households and those for general (non-BPL) households.

Specifically, the purpose of the book is to examine the extent to which rural houses provide living space for rural population settled in the hilly regions, the quality-cum-durability of rural houses constructed under government-sponsored housing schemes and local calamities like earthquake, landslide that affect the people settled in the hilly regions, the reasons why some houses sanctioned under Government schemes have not been started/completed, and why some houses have remained unutilized/abandoned/transferred, the use of local resources in construction of houses, and the scope for employment of rural people in construction of houses, and the role of Panchayati Raj Institutions in implementation of rural housing programmes.

The purpose is to test the conjectures that the execution of rural housing schemes ensures utilization of local resources, including manpower, and simultaneously promotes rural infrastructure; provision of Government-sponsored rural housing programmes uplifts the housing condition and ensures security of the rural income-poor people settled in rural hilly regions of the state; provision for living space through rural housing schemes may discourage forced migration of rural people; involvement of rural people though Panchayati Raj Institutions (PRIs) in decisions regarding location of rural houses may ensure the success of Rural Housing Schemes.

The study tools and major objectives at different levels are shown in Flow Chart 2.1.

In Uttarakhand, there are two geographical regions, namely, Kumaon and Garhwal. We have covered both the regions. From each region, we selected two Districts. Thus, we covered four districts in Uttarakhand. From each district, we selected two blocks, one developed and the other underdeveloped. From each block, we selected a minimum of five villages based on random sampling method applying listing of villages in alphabetical order. Some additional villages were selected to compensate sample loss in case the targets have not been fulfilled. From each village, we selected 10 beneficiary households. Thus, we selected four districts, eight blocks, 54 (including additional sample) villages, and 400 households. The sample structure for the study is shown in Flow Chart 2.2.

We have also covered state, district, block, and village level functionaries of housing programmes. The sampling procedure at each level is shown in Flow Chart 2.3.

Flow Chart 2.1: Different Activities and Coverage of the Study

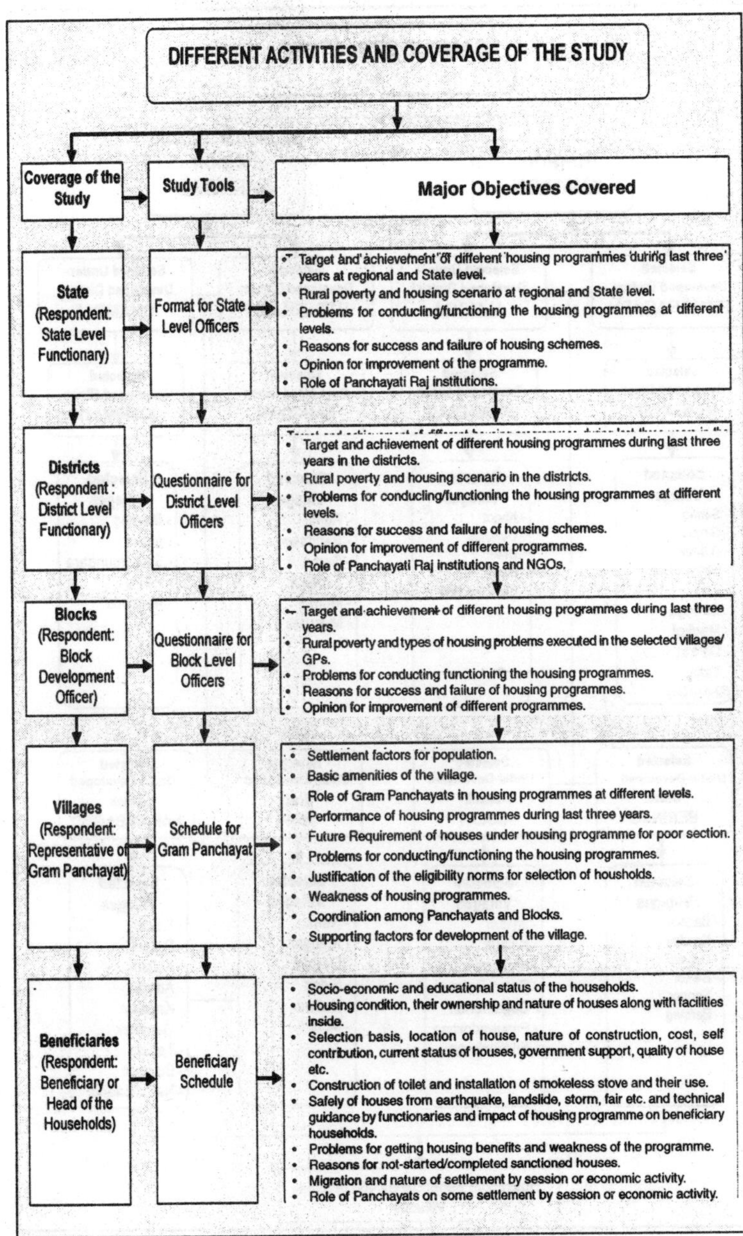

Flow Chart 2.2 : Sample Structure

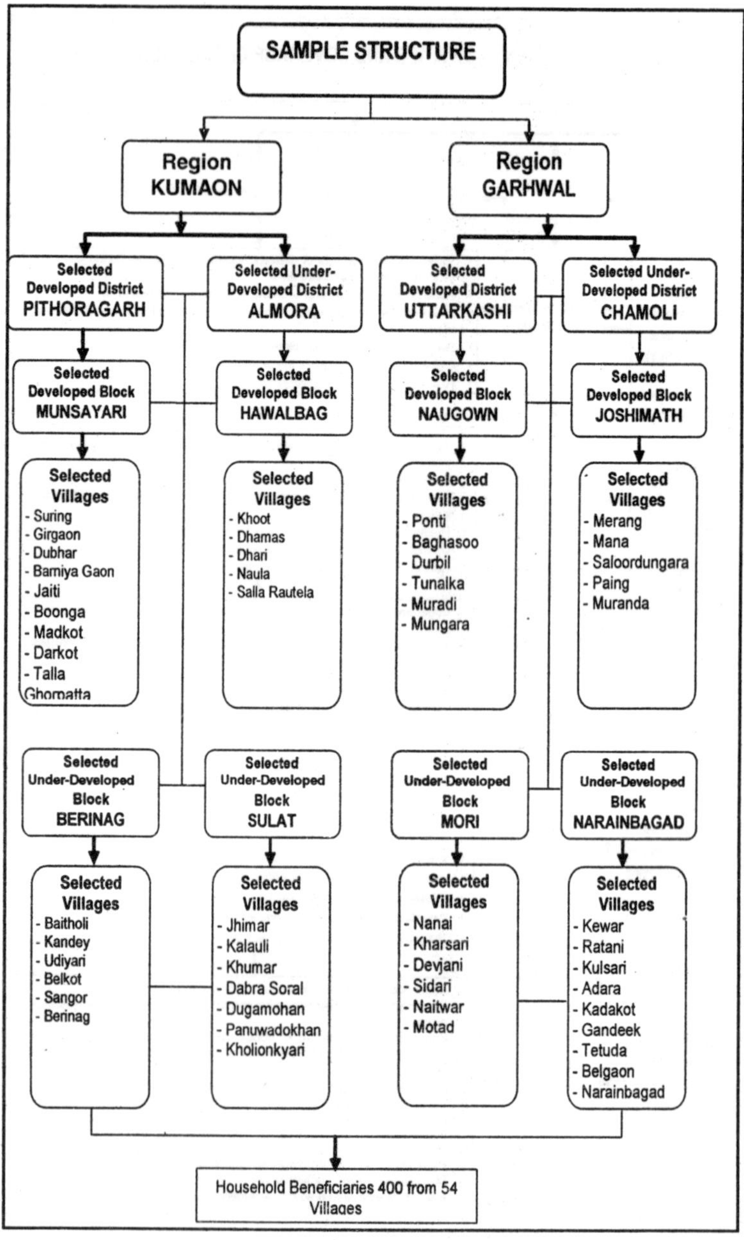

Flow Chart 2.3 : Sample Procedure

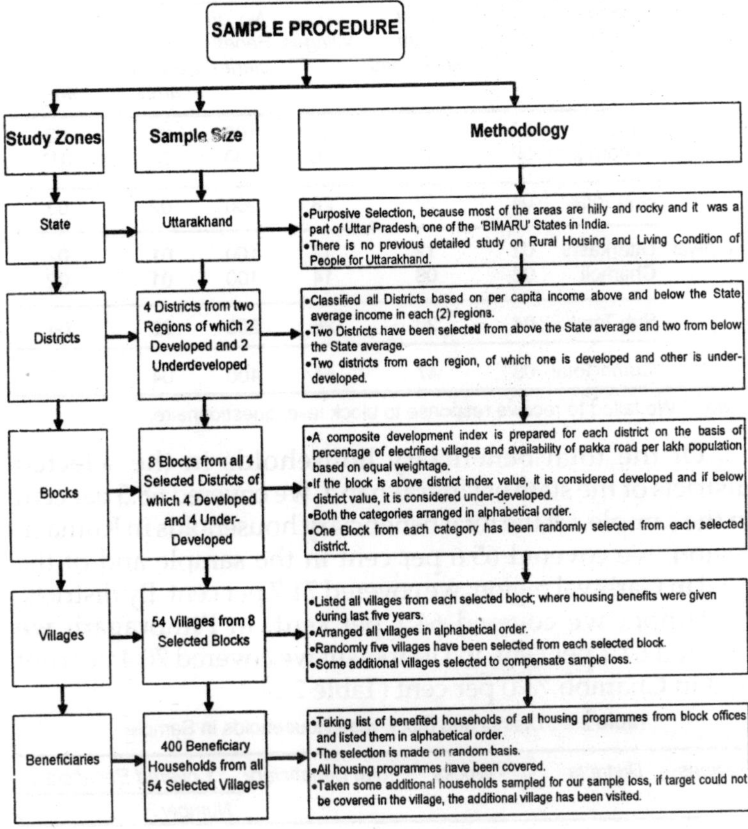

2.2 Selected Zone : Observations on Housing

We covered both the regions, namely, Kumaon and Garhwal, of the state of Uttarakhand. We covered two districts from each region, from Kumaon the districts are Almora and Pithoragarh, and from Garhwal region, the districts are Uttarkashi and Chamoli. In total, we covered eight blocks, selecting two from each district. We covered a total of 47 Gram Panchayats, 54 villages from those Panchyats. We interviewed a total of 11 functionaries from the Government of Uttarakhand at the levels of block and district. We covered 400 beneficiary households (Table 2.1).

Table 2.1: Region and District-wise Coverage of Areas and Targets

Regions	*Districts*	*Number of Blocks*	*No. of Gram Panchayats*	*No. of Villages*	*No. of Beneficiaries*	*No. of District Functionaries*	*No. of Block Functionaries*
Kumaun	Almora	02	11	12	100	01	02
	Pithoragarh	02	16	16	100	01	01*
	Sub Total	04	27	28	200	02	03
Garhwal	Uttarkashi	02	12	12	100	01	02
	Chamoli	02	08	14	100	01	02
	Sub Total	04	20	26	200	02	04
	Grand Total	08	47	54	400	04	07

Note : * We failed to receive response to block level questionnaire.

Of the total beneficiary households in the selected districts of the state of Uttarakhand, we covered 68.5 per cent in the sample. Of the total beneficiary households in Kumaon region, we covered 65.6 per cent in the sample and of the total in Garhwal region, we covered 71.7 per cent. By districts, in Almora we covered 64.1 per cent, in Pithoragarh we covered 67.1 per cent, in Uttarkashi we covered 70.4 per cent and in Chamoli 73.0 per cent (Table 2.2).

Table 2.2 : District and Block-wise Households in Sample

Regions	*Districts*	*Blocks*	*Total Beneficiary*	*Covered Beneficiary*	
				Number	*%*
Kumaun	Almora	Hawalbag	59	50	84.7
		Sult	97	50	51.5
		Total	156	100	64.1
	Pithoragarh	Munshiyari	76	50	65.8
		Berinag	73	50	68.5
		Total	149	100	67.1
	Sub-Total Regions		305	200	65.6
Garahwal	Uttarkashi	Mori	61	50	82.0
		Naugown	81	50	61.7
		Total	142	100	70.4
	Chamoli	Narain Bagad	54	50	92.6
		Joshimath	83	50	60.2
		Total	137	100	73.0
		Sub-Total Regions	279	200	71.7
		Grand Total	584	400	68.5

Of the block total beneficiaries, in the respective districts in Kumaon region in Uttarakhand, we covered the beneficiary households as follows :

In Hawalbag block in Almora, we covered 84.7 per cent of the total beneficiary households, which was 51.5 per cent for Sult in Almora; in Munshiyari block in Pithoragarh district, we covered 65.8 per cent of the total beneficiaries that was 68.5 per cent in Berinag block of Pithoragarh (Table 2.3).

Table 2.3 : District, Block and Village-wise Total and Covered Number of Beneficiary Households in Kumaon Region of Uttarakhand

Districts	*Blocks*	*Name of Villages*	*Total Beneficiary Households*	*Covered Beneficiary Households*	
				Number	*%*
Almora	Hawalbag	Khoont	08	07	87.5
		Dhamash	17	14	82.4
		Dhari	11	10	90.9
		Naula	13	12	92.3
		Salla Rautela	10	07	70.0
		Block Total	59	50	84.7
	Sult	Jhimar	17	15	88.2
		Kalauli	04	02	50.0
		Khumar	11	01	9.1
		Dabarasoral	21	15	71.4
		Dugamohan	11	05	45.5
		Panuadokhan	17	05	29.4
		Kholiyo Kyari	16	07	43.8
		Block Total	97	50	51.5
		District Total	156	100	64.1
Pithoragarh	Munshiyari	Suring	05	03	60.0
		Girgown	14	08	57.1
		Dhumar	08	06	75.0
		Barniyagown	04	02	50.0
		Jaitee	07	05	71.4
		Boonga	11	07	63.6
		Madkot	09	06	66.7
		Darkot	05	03	60.0
		Talla Ghorpatta	06	05	83.3
		Malla Ghorpatta	07	5	71.4
		Block Total	76	50	65.8
	Berinag	Baithauli	06	04	66.7
		Kande	08	05	62.5
		Udiyari	07	04	57.1
		Belkot	17	13	76.5
		Sangor	22	16	72.7
		Berinag	13	08	61.5
		Block Total	73	50	68.5
		District Total	149	100	67.1
Region Kumaon Total			305	200	65.6

Of the block total beneficiaries in the respective districts in Garhwal region in Uttarakhand, we covered the beneficiary households as follows:

In Mori block in Uttarkashi district we covered 66.7 per cent of the total beneficiary households, which was 61.7 per cent for Naugaon. In Narain Bagad block in Chamoli district, we covered 92.6 per cent of the total beneficiaries that was 60.2 per cent of the total beneficiaries for Joshimath block in Chamoli (Table 2.4).

Table 2.4 : Total and Covered Number of Beneficiary Households in Garhwal Region of Uttarakhand

Districts	*Blocks*	*Name of Villages*	*Total Beneficiary Households*	*Covered Beneficiary Households*	
				Number	*%*
Uttarkashi	Mori	Nanai	12	4	33.3
		Kharsari	6	6	100
		Devjani	22	21	95.5
		Sidari	5	5	100
		Naitwar	10	10	100
		Motard	6	4	66.7
		Block Total	61	50	82
	Naugaon	Pontee	20	14	70
		Baghasoo	7	6	85.7
		Durbil	37	13	35.1
		Tunalka	6	6	100
		Moradi	8	8	100
		Mungara	3	3	100
		Block Total	81	50	61.7
	District Total		142	100	100
Chamoli	Narain Bagad	Kewar	14	13	92.9
		Ratani	1	1	100
		Kulsari	12	11	91.7
		Adara	10	10	100
		Karakot	7	7	100
		Gandik	3	1	33.3
		Narain Bagad	2	2	100
		Tetuda	1	1	100
		Bergown	4	4	100
		Block Total	54	50	92.6
	Joshimath	Merang	4	3	75
		Mana	37	17	45.9
		Salurdungra	22	15	68.2
		Paing	15	10	66.7
		Moranda	5	5	100
		Block Total	83	50	60.2
	District Total		137	100	100
Region Garhwal Total			279	200	279

2.3 Characteristics of Selected Districts

District : Pithoragarh

District Pithoragarh in Kumaon region situated in the Himalayas has borders with China and Nepal. We selected two development blocks, Munsyari and Berinag, from this district which lie in the north and central regions respectively. In terms of infrastructural facilities Munsyari lies much below the average of the district while Berinag is among the developed blocks. According to the 2001 Census, the population densities of Munsyari and Berinag were 18 and 252 persons per sq. km. respectively.

District : Almora

Almora is an old district in the Kumaon region. According to the 2001 Census, the rural population as percentage of the total population of Almora was 93.4, the population density 171, and the rate of increase of population per annum (1991-2001) was 3.67 per cent. The average number of households in both rural and urban areas was five. There are a total of 11 development blocks out of which two blocks, namely Salt and Hawalbag, were selected. The topography of this region is similar to that of the Garhwal region and its borders also touch the Garhwal Mandal.

District : Uttarkashi

The borders of district Uttarkashi touch countries like China, Tibet and the State of Himachal Pradesh in the north; district Chamoli in the east, Tehri Garhwal in the south and Dehradun in the west. According to the 2001 Census, the total population of this district was 2,95,013 which was 3.46 per cent of the population of the State of Uttarakhand. The urban population of the district was only 7.8 per cent. The density of population was 37 per sq. km. Between 1991 and

2001, the population in the district increased by 23.07 per cent. The literacy rate of the district was 65.7 per cent, of males 83.6 per cent while of females 46.7 per cent. We selected two blocks from the district, Mori and Naugaon. The per cent of people residing in rural areas in these two blocks were 93.2 and 100.0 respectively. Mori block was backward while Naugaon was developed.

District : Chamoli

District Chamoli was formed on 24 February, 1960 when tehsil Chamoli, district Pauri, was made a separate district. The entire district lies in the mountainous region. On its north lies Tibet, to its south is Pauri, to its east are Almora and Pithoragarh, and in the west is Uttarkashi, Tehri and Rudraprayag district. In the east of the district which comprises districts like Mana, Niti, Gamsali, there is strong influence of Tibetan culture. According to the Census 2001, the population of the entire district was 3,70,359 of which 49.6 per cent were males. Of the total population, 86.3 per cent lived in rural areas. In the rural areas there were 65,216 houses in which 3,19,656 people used to reside. Thus, on average, five people used to reside in each house. The Scheduled Castes and Scheduled Tribes made up 21.07 per cent of the total population of the district. The sex ratio was 1017 females per 1000 males. The population density was 49 persons per square kilometre. The majority of the population in the district depended upon agriculture for their livelihood, sheep rearing. We selected two blocks, Joshimath and Narayan Bagar, from the nine development blocks. While Joshimath was developed, Narayan Bagar was underdeveloped.

2.4 Socio-Economic Profile : Selected Districts and Uttarakhand

In Uttarakhand, following Census 2001, there was low

density of population (159 per sq. km.) with a literacy rate of 71.6 per cent, male literacy rate being 83.3 and female literacy 59.6. The percentage of SC population stood at 17.9 and that of ST 3.0. Average size of family stood at 5.3. The percentage of urban population was 25.7. Work participation ratio was 36.9 per cent, the percentage of main workers 27.4, marginal workers 9.6 and non-workers 63.1. The percentage of BPL households stood at 47.2 and credit-deposit ratio at 39.0.

50.1 per cent of the total workers in Uttarakhand were engaged as cultivators, 8.3 per cent as agricultural labourers, and 2.3 per cent as workers in household industries. The rest, 39.3 per cent, were non-classified workers. There were variations in workers engaged in occupations by percentages by gender and by regions.

Of the total households in the selected districts, 47.3 per cent were BPL. Of the total households in SCs, 30.5 per cent were BPL, which was as high as 65.9 per cent within general castes, and as low as 2.1 per cent from STs and 1.8 per cent from OBCs. The distribution of households in the selected districts shows uniformity for each district, each showing around 47.0 per cent. Within each district, the households coming under BPL as percentage of all households were more in case of general castes relative to SCs, STs and OBCs (Table 2.5).

Table 2.5 : Poverty Scenario in Selected Districts by Castes

Districts		*BPL Households*					*Total Households*
		SC	*ST*	*OBC*	*Others*	*Total BPL*	
Uttarkashi	No	8998	335	405	18747	28485	60525
	%	31.6	1.2	1.4	65.8	47.1	100.0
Chamoli	No	8370	664	358	22992	32384	68151
	%	25.8	2.1	1.1	71.0	47.5	100.0
Pithoragarh	No	14383	2486	1600	25660	44129	93732
	%	32.6	5.6	3.6	58.1	47.1	100.0
Almora	No	18811	0	594	41848	60659	127458
	%	31.0	0.0	1.0	69.0	47.6	100.0
Total	No	50562	3485	2957	109247	165657	349866
	%	30.5	2.1	1.8	65.9	47.3	100.0

Note : The per cent on castes groups calculated on total BPL households and per cent of total BPL households calculated on total households.

Source : Data provided by DRDA of concerned districts.

Of total BPL households in the selected districts following BPL survey 2002, 2.7 per cent were houseless, which was 1.9 per cent in Uttarkashi (as per cent of total BPL households), 2.1 per cent in Chamoli, 2.6 per cent in Pithoragarh and 3.3 per cent in Almora. Of total SC BPL households, 6.3 per cent were houseless, which was 6.7 per cent for STs, 2.2 for OBCs and 5.1 per cent for General castes (Table 2.6).

2.4.1 Poverty and Houseless Households in Selected Gram Panchayats

Comparing BPL survey 2002 with that of 1998 we find increase in poverty over the period by percentage of households and population. By households, the percentage increase in BPL was 19.2 for the sample regions and by population (in sample) it was by 16.4. By regions, for Garhwal, the percentage increase in BPL by households was 22.2 and by population 17.5, while for Kumaon, by households the percentage increase in BPL was 14.7 and by population 15.0. By districts, each of Uttarkashi and Chamoli in Garhwal region showed increase in poverty (BPL list) in 2002 over 1998, while in Kumaon region, Almora showed increase and Pithoragarh showed reduction in BPL. The size of households in Garhwal got reduced from 4.7 to 4.5, while for Kumaon it remained the same at 5.0.

Of total BPL households in district Uttarkashi, 3.2 per cent were houseless and 12.5 per cent had *Kutcha* houses; the respective percentages were 2.7 and 11.0 for district Chamoli, 4.3 and 8.9 in district Almora, 7.5 and 34.3 in district Pithoragarh. For the region Garhwal, these percentages were 3.0 and 12.0 respectively while for the region Kumaon these percentages were 5.2 and 16.2. Of the total sample BPL households following information provided by block offices, 3.9 per cent were houseless and 13.6 per cent had *Kutcha* houses (Table 2.7).

Table 2.6 : Houseless Households in Selected Districts based on BPL Survey 2002

Districts		*SC*		*ST*		*OBC*		*Others*		*Total*	
		House-less	*Total BPL*	*House-less*	*Total BPL*	*House-less*	*Total BPL*	*House-less*	*Total BPL*	*House-less*	*Total BPL*
Uttarkashi	No.	444	8998	13	335	0	405	714	18747	1171	60525
	%	4.9	100.0	3.9	100.0	0.0	100.0	3.8	100.0	1.9	100.0
Chamoli	No.	446	8370	16	664	13	358	972	22992	1447	68151
	%	5.3	100.0	2.4	100.0	3.6	100.0	4.2	100.0	2.1	100.0
Pithoragarh	No.	901	14383	205	2486	52	1600	1274	25660	2432	93732
	%	6.3	100.0	8.2	100.0	3.3	100.0	5.0	100.0	2.6	100.0
Almora	No.	1386	18811	0	0	0	594	2570	41848	4256	127458
	%	7.4	100.0	–	–	0.0	100.0	6.1	100.0	3.3	100.0
Total	No.	3177	50562	234	3485	65	2957	5530	109247	9306	349866
	%	6.3	100.0	6.7	100.0	2.2	100.0	5.1	100.0	2.7	100.0

Source : Data provided by DRDA of concerned districts.

Table 2.7: Housing Status of BPL Households in Selected Gram Panchayats

Regions	*Districts*	*Castes*	*Housing Status*				*Total BPL Households*	
			Houseless		*Kutcha*			
			No.	*%*	*No.*	*%*	*No.*	*%*
Garhwal	Uttarkashi	SC	25	4.3	47	8.1	581	100.0
		ST	0	–	0	–	0	–
		OBC	0	0.0	23	21.5	107	100.0
		Others	18	2.7	98	14.8	661	100.0
		Total	43	3.2	168	12.5	1349	100.0
	Chamoli	SC	9	6.9	22	16.9	130	100.0
		ST	0	0.0	11	8.1	136	100.0
		OBC	0	–	0	–	0	–
		Others	8	2.2	37	10.0	369	100.0
		Total	17	2.7	70	11.0	635	100.0
	Total Region		60	3.0	238	12.0	1984	100.0
Kumaun	Almora	SC	14	4.0	35	10.1	347	100.0
		ST	0	–	0	–	0	–
		OBC	0	0.0	0	0.0	1	100.0
		Others	23	4.5	42	8.2	514	100.0
		Total	37	4.3	77	8.9	862	100.0
	Pithoragarh	SC	14	7.5	53	28.3	187	100.0
		ST	0	0.0	0	0.0	1	100.0
		OBC	0	–	0	–	0	–
		Others	12	7.5	66	41.5	159	100.0
		Total	26	7.5	119	34.3	347	100.0
	Total Region		63	5.2	196	16.2	1209	100.0
	Total sampled		123	3.9	434	13.6	3193	100.0

Note : * The data of Munshiyari's block not included because non-availability of data from block office.
Source : Information provided by selected block offices.

2.5 Housing Programmes in Selected Districts

We found Indira Awaas Yojana as the major housing scheme being implemented in all the selected districts. The other housing schemes include credit-cum-subsidy for rural housing and Pradhan Mantri Gramin Awaas Yojana. A large number of houses under Bhuskhalan Awaas Yojana were being implemented in the remote hilly region, which was part of the IAY scheme. This scheme is mentioned in this chapter as 'other category'. The state government introduced a housing scheme, namely, Dindayal Uttarakhand Awaas Yojana (DUAY). The major running housing schemes are being shown in Flow Chart 2.4.

Flow Chart 2.4 : Rural Housing Schemes in Uttarakhand.

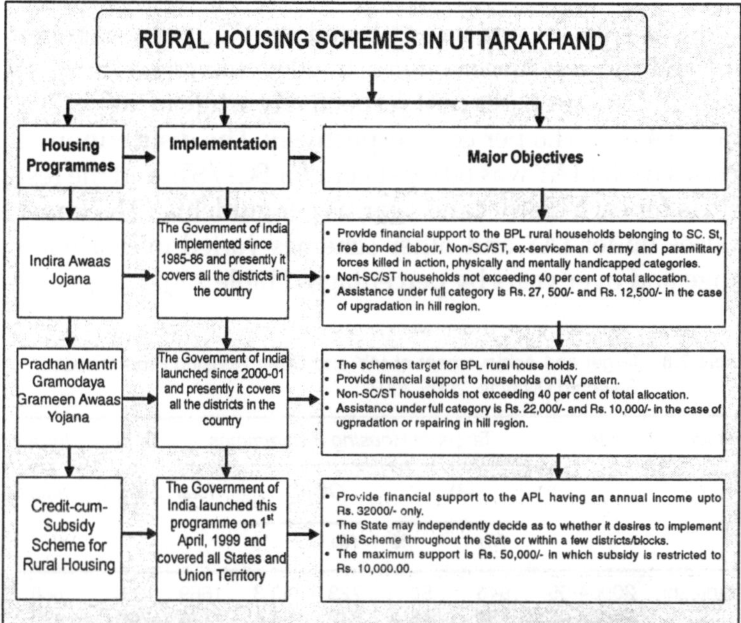

2.5.1 Physical and Financial Progress of IAY in Uttarakhand

Of all the houses targeted under IAY in India in 2006-07, the achievement rate was 102.7 per cent. Of total achievement, women were allotted 72.5 per cent. By castes, SCs got 42.4 per cent and STs 12.5 per cent. By land ownership, landless households got 37.4 per cent of the houses under IAY in 2006-07.

Of the total fund for housing under IAY in 2006-07 in India, 82.3 per cent was utilized. Of total allocation, the central share was 75.0 per cent and the state's share 25.0 per cent in 2006-07. Of total release of fund, central share was 61.5 per cent and the rest state's share.

Considered on a span of last three years (2004-07), we calculated the targets (as percentages) of households under housing programmes, namely, IAY and others, which are as follows at district level :

In 2004-05, the target distributed was 72.3 per cent under IAY and the rest under others. In 2006, the ratios (targets) were 35.3 and 64.7 per cent respectively while in 2006-07, it was 35.4 and 64.6 per cent respectively. The distribution of houses under IAY was 60.0 per cent for SCs/STs and the rest others for each district and year, as per guideline. The target houses under IAY and other schemes varied over a wide range and over years by percentages (Table 2.8).

Table 2.8 : Target and Achievement of IAY and Other Housing Programmes in Selected Districts, 2005-2007

Districts	*Years*	*Target of Housing Programmes*					*Target for SC/ST*	*Target for Others*
		IAY		*Other*		*Total*		
		No.	*%*	*No.*	*%*			
Uttarkashi	20004-05	946	56.7	723	43.3	1669	1001	668
	20005-06	534	45.4	642	54.6	1176	706	470
	20006-07	293	37.4	491	62.6	784	470	314
Chamoli	20004-05	784	76.0	248	24.0	1032	619	413
	20005-06	392	36.5	681	63.5	1073	644	429
	20006-07	236	19.1	999	80.9	1235	741	494
Pithoragarh	20004-05	529	61.0	339	39.0	868	521	347
	20005-06	252	37.7	417	62.3	669	402	268
	20006-07	268	50.0	268	50.0	536	322	215
Almora	20004-05	2720	81.9	602	18.1	3322	1993	1329
	20005-06	362	25.0	1085	75.0	1447	868	579
	20006-07	310	53.7	267	46.3	577	346	231
Total	20004-05	1245	72.3	478	27.7	1723	1034	689
	20005-06	385	35.3	706	64.7	1091	655	437
	20006-07	277	35.4	506	64.6	783	470	313

Note : The DRDA administration reported that the target, allocation and achievement data are same.

Source : Data provided by DRDA of concerned districts.

3

Housing Conditions of Households

We present in this chapter the housing conditions of the beneficiary households settled in rural Uttarakhand. The governments functioning at three layers, centre, state, and the Panchayati Raj Institutions, are seen as the agencies to ensure housing and related basic needs of life for human living. We covered 47 Panchayat representatives, four district level functionaries, eight block level functionaries, and 400 households benefited from different rural housing schemes. We covered Uttarakhand by two administrative regions, and selected 200 households from each region. We selected two districts from each region and selected 100 households from each district.

3.1 Profile of Beneficiary Households

The caste composition of the sample beneficiary households shows that 51.3 per cent were SCs, 10.8 per cent STs, 13.0 per cent OBCs and 25.0 per cent general castes. The presence of OBCs by percentage was most in Uttarkashi district and nil in Pithoragarh, and negligible in Almora and Chamoli districts. STs in the sample were nil in Almora and Uttarkashi, and present to some extent (31.0 per cent of total STs in sample) in Chamoli district. The districts Pithoragarh and Almora were selected from Kumaun region; the districts Uttarkashi and Chamoli were from Garhwal region (Table 3.1).

Table 3.1: Beneficiary Households by Castes

Regions	*Districts*		*SC*	*ST*	*OBC*	*General*	*Total*
Kumaun	Pithoragarh	No.	58	12	0	30	100
		%	58.0	12.0	0.0	30.0	100.0
	Almora	No.	65	0	1	34	100
		%	65.0	0.0	1.0	34.0	100.0
	Sub-Total	**No.**	**123**	**12**	**1**	**64**	**200**
		%	**61.5**	**6.0**	**0.5**	**32.0**	**100.0**
Garhwal	Uttarkashi	No.	44	0	50	6	100
		%	44.0	0.0	50.0	6.0	100.0
	Chamoli	No.	38	31	1	30	100
		%	38.0	31.0	1.0	30.0	100.0
	Sub-Total	**No.**	**82**	**31**	**51**	**36**	**200**
		%	**41.0**	**15.5**	**25.5**	**18.0**	**100.0**
Total Sample		No.	205	43	52	100	400
		%	51.3	10.8	13.0	25.0	100.0

Source : Field Survey, 2008.

Of all the beneficiary households in the sample, 56.0 per cent were from IAY, 20.3 per cent from CCSRHP and the rest from other schemes like Bhuskhalan Awaas Yojana, and Pradhan Mantri Grameen Awaas Yojana. Of the sample beneficiary households under IAY, 61.5 per cent were from Kumaun and 50.5 per cent were from Garhwal region (Table 3.2).

Of all the respondent beneficiary households, 26.5 per cent were illiterates, 32.8 per cent were below primary level, 3.0 per cent had education above intermediate level and 0.3 per cent had technical education.

The major occupations of households were labour (41.8 per cent), followed by cultivation (17.3 per cent) and other small seasonal/temporary/traditional activities, like animal husbandry, weaving/sewing, business and service (Table 3.3).

Table 3.2 : Beneficiary Households by Housing Programmes

Regions	*Districts*		*IAY*	*CCSRHP*	*Others**	*Total*
Kumaun	Pithoragarh	No.	54	25	21	100
		%	54.0	25.0	21.0	100.0
	Almora	No.	69	20	11	100
		%	69.0	20.0	11.0	100.0
	Sub-Total	**No.**	**123**	**45**	**32**	**200**
		%	**61.5**	**22.5**	**16.0**	**100.0**
Garhwal	Uttarkashi	No.	67	17	16	100
		%	67.0	17.0	16.0	100.0
	Chamoli	No.	34	19	47	100
		%	34.0	19.0	47.0	100.0
	Sub-Total	**No.**	**101**	**36**	**63**	**200**
		%	**50.5**	**18.0**	**31.5**	**100.0**
Total Sample		No.	224	81	95	400
		%	56.0	20.3	23.8	100.0

Note : One household was double benefited by Bhuskhalan Awaas Yojana and CCSRHP.

* Bhuskhalan Awaas Yojna, Pradhan Mantri Grameen Awaas Yojana.

Source : Field Survey, 2008.

Table 3.3 : Occupations of Households as Respondents

Occupations	*Pithoragarh*	*Almora*	*Uttarkashi*	*Chamoli*	*Total*	
					No.	*%*
No Occupation	0	1	1	1	3	0.8
Cultivation	16	11	34	8	69	17.3
Animal Husbandry	3	2	2	6	13	3.3
Govt. Service	5	0	0	0	5	1.3
Pvt. Service	3	5	2	3	13	3.3
Skilled Labour	2	5	1	3	11	2.8
Manual Labour	38	47	45	37	167	41.8
Business	6	11	0	5	22	5.5
Traditional Work	3	4	1	1	9	2.3
Housewives	10	11	12	15	48	12.0
Pensioner	5	3	0	2	10	2.5
Weaving/Sewing	6	0	2	18	26	6.5
Study	3	0	0	1	4	1.0
Total Sample	100	100	100	100	400	100.0

Source : Field Survey, 2008.

3.2 Settlement and Rootedness of Households on the Hills

Most of the facilities required by households for living on the links were available like physical and social infrastructure, communications and services, public administration, and health-related facilities.

The major reasons for settlement of population on the hills were availability of water, fertile land for agriculture, availability and suitability of space for animal husbandry, and forestry for hunting. The other reasons cited were climate/temperature, opportunities for horticulture, woolen work, and availability of wood (Flow Chart 3.1).

Flow Chart 3.1: Reasons for Settlement of Population on the Hills (As Mentioned by Functionaries in Gram Panchayats)

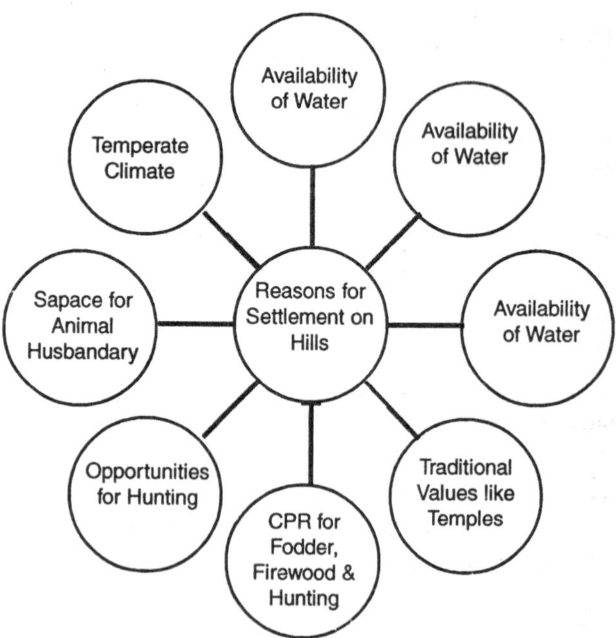

Source : Field Survey, 2008.

Most of the households (95.8 per cent) were settled in rural Uttarakhand by birth. Absence of employment opportunities was the most important reason for migration. The other reasons were absence of educational institutions in the locality, and unwelcome relations with neighbours in the locality (Box 3.1).

Box 3.1: Reasons for Migration

Reasons
Absence of Educational Institutions
Absence of Employment Opportunities
Presence of working members in family
Unwelcome relations with neighbours
Absence of Transport
Absence of Educational Centres and Employment Opportunities
Employment and family members already working here

Source: Field Survey, 2008.

3.3 Education, Occupation and Income of Beneficiary Households

By districts, of total population from sample in Pithoragarh, 16.8 per cent were illiterate, which were 19.5 per cent in Almora, 25.5 per cent in Uttarkashi and 10.7 per cent in Chamoli. In these districts, female illiteracy was more than male illiteracy; higher education above school level was rare.

Of the total population in the sample, 18.2 per cent were illiterate, with higher female illiteracy. 24.7 per cent got education up to primary level and 9.9 per cent were just-literate. Only 0.3 per cent got graduation and above. Of the SC population in the sample, 20.1 per cent were illiterate, which were 8.2 per cent from STs, 30.3 per cent from OBCs and 12.4 per cent from General castes. In all cases, female illiteracy was more than male illiteracy. There was no individual from population in STs who had got graduation. Higher education in general, over all the castes and gender, was rare for the population from the sample. Of all the population in the age bracket 6 to 14 in the selected region, school going boys and girls were respectively 95.1 and 94.4 per cent. The categories like 'never school going' and 'dropout' were very negligible.

Of total population from the sample households, 38.7 per cent constituted working section and 61.3 per cent non-working section. Of the total working population, 25.4 per cent were engaged in agriculture, 34.5 per cent were engaged as labourers, 6.7 per cent were engaged in animal husbandry, and others were engaged in business, traditional works and services (Table 3.4).

Table 3.4 : Working Population by Nature of Occupations

Occupations	*Total Sample*
Agriculture	25.4
Animal Husbandry	6.7
Govt. Service	2.7
Private Service	6.0
Skilled Labour	9.2
Manual Labour	34.5
Business	4.7
Traditional Business	2.2
Large Business	0.4
Others	8.3
Total	812 (100.0)

Source : Field Survey, 2008.

Of the total working population, 74.5 per cent were male and 25.5 per cent female. Of the female workers, 32.9 per cent were engaged in agriculture, 23.2 per cent engaged in animal husbandry and 17.9 per cent worked as labourers (both skilled and unskilled). Of the male workers, 40.2 per cent were engaged in labour works, 22.8 per cent engaged in agriculture and rest in multiple works like business and services that showed 'work compulsions' and not 'job diversifications'.

Of the working population engaged as labourers, most

were from SCs. Of the SC workers in different works, the prominent ones were labour and agriculture. Of the working population from STs, and OBCs and general castes most were engaged in wage-labour, and agriculture.

The major activities for occupational support of the settled population in Uttarakhand were cultivation, wage-labour, animal husbandry and dairy work, services, woolen work and business. The other activities that provided support were tourism, collection of herbal grass and plants having medicinal value and fishing.

3.3.1 Income of Population from Sample Households

The average income per month of the working population from the sample in 2008 stood at Rs. 1281, that varied between the range of Rs. 1072 (minimum for Uttarkashi) and Rs. 1555 (maximum for Pithoragarh). The average income stood between the maximum at Rs. 5645 from government services and Rs. 526 from animal husbandry at the minimum. The work that provided second highest income opportunity was large business, while agriculture provided little opportunity for high income (Table 3.5).

Table 3.5 : Average Monthly Income of Working Population by Occupations

Occupations	Total (Rs.)
Agriculture	597
Animal Husbandry	526
Govt. Service	5645
Private Service	2233
Skilled Labour	1300
Manual Labour	1344
Business	1811
Traditional Business	778
Large Business	3467
Others	1322
Total Monthly Income	1281

Source : Field Survey, 2008.

Per capita income per annam. for the population from the sample households was estimated at Rs. 5,945 that varied between Rs. 7,372 at the maximum for the district Chamoli and minimum at Rs. 4,564 for the district Almora. Of the average income (PCI) across castes, the lowest was for OBCs (Rs. 4,914) and highest at Rs. 10,244 for STs. Income per household per annum for STs stood at Rs. 42,642 (maximum) and Rs. 24, 854 for OBCs (minimum) as estimated in 2008. There were district-wise variations in these estimates (Table 3.6).

Table 3.6 : Per Capita Income and Annual Income Per Household by Districts and Castes

Districts	*Total Population*	*Total Annual Income (Rs.)*	*PCI (Rs.)*
Pithoragarh	506	3564012	7044
Almora	626	2857200	4564
Uttarkashi	498	2598600	5218
Chamoli	470	3465000	7372
Total HHs.	2100	12484812	5945

Castes	*Pop.*	*Total Annual Income (Rs.)*	*PCI (Rs.)*	*Per HH. Income (Rs.)*
SC	1130	5563200	4923	27138
ST	179	1833612	10244	42642
OBC	263	1292400	4914	24854
General	528	3795600	7189	37956
Total	2100	12484812	5945	31212

Source : Field Survey, 2008.

Of all the sample households, 39.3 per cent earned income p.a. between Rs. 20,000. and Rs. 32,000. One quarter of the households earned income p.a. between Rs. 10,000. and Rs. 20,000. Per annum income per household exceeded Rs. 50,000 for 13.1 per cent of the households. Thus, 86.9 per cent of the households earned income p.a. below Rs. 50,000.

Of the sample households, 56.0 per cent were under IAY, 20.2 per cent under CCSRHP and the rest under other schemes. Of all the beneficiary households under IAY, 40.6 per cent earned between Rs. 20,000 and Rs. 32,000 p.a. and 9.3 per cent earned income p.a. above Rs. 50,000. The percentage of households under IAY earning less than Rs. 20,000 came to be 34.4. Of the beneficiary households under CCSRHP, 35.8 per cent earned income p.a. between Rs. 20,000 and Rs. 32,000 Between Rs. 32,000 and Rs. 50,000 there were 29.6 per cent of households under CCSRHP. 20.9 per cent of households under CCSRHP earned income above Rs. 50,000 p.a. (Table 3.7).

Table 3.7 : Annual Household Income by Beneficiary Households under Housing Programmes

Income Brackets (Rs.)		*IAY*	*CCSRHP*	*Others*	*Total*
Up to 10000	No.	10	0	3	13
	%	4.5	0.0	3.2	3.3
10000 to 20000	No.	67	11	23	101
	%	29.9	13.6	24.2	25.3
20000 to 32000	No.	91	29	37	157
	%	40.6	35.8	38.9	39.3
32000 to 50000	No.	35	24	18	77
	%	15.6	29.6	18.9	19.3
50000 to 75000	No.	16	10	11	37
	%	7.1	12.3	11.6	9.3
More than 75000	No.	5	7	3	15
	%	2.2	8.6	3.2	3.8
Total	No.	224	81	95	400
	%	100.0	100.0	100.0	100.0

Source : Field Survey, 2008.

Of all the households under IAY, 34.4 per cent had annual income less than Rs. 20,000 that is, 65.6 per cent had income p.a. more than Rs. 20,000. In a district like Chamoli, the household income p.a., as IAY beneficiaries, was more than Rs. 20,000 for 85.3 per cent of district total beneficiary households. Of all the beneficiary households under CCSRHP, 56.6 per cent of the households had income Per annum more than Rs. 32,000. Of the beneficiary households under other housing schemes, 72.6 per cent had income p.a. more than Rs. 20,000. (Table 3.8).

Table 3.8 : Annual Household Income by Housing Programmes by Districts

Programme	*Annual (Income Rs.)*		*Pithora-garh*	*Almora*	*Uttar-kashi*	*Chamoli*	*Total*
Indira Awaas Yojana	Up to 20,000	No.	23	24	25	5	77
		%	42.6	34.8	37.3	14.7	34.4
	More than 20,000	No.	31	45	42	29	147
		%	57.4	65.2	62.7	85.3	65.6
	Total	**No.**	**54**	**69**	**67**	**34**	**224**
		%	**100.0**	**100.0**	**100.0**	**100.0**	**100.0**
Credit-cum-Subsidy Rural Housing Programme	Up to 32,000	No.	8	9	13	10	40
		%	32.0	45.0	76.5	52.6	49.4
	More than 32,000	No.	17	11	4	9	41
		%	68.0	55.0	23.5	47.4	50.6
	Total	**No.**	**25**	**20**	**17**	**19**	**81**
		%	**100.0**	**100.0**	**100.0**	**100.0**	**100.0**
Others	Up to 20,000	No.	9	6	3	8	26
		%	42.9	54.5	18.8	17.0	27.4
	More than 20,000	No.	12	5	13	39	69
		%	57.1	45.5	81.3	83.0	72.6
	Total	**No.**	**21**	**11**	**16**	**47**	**95**
		%	**100.0**	**100.0**	**100.0**	**100.0**	100.0

Source : Field Survey, 2008.

3.4 Households Owning Land and Assets

While 13.3 per cent of the beneficiary households were landless, 42.0 per cent had landholding less than 0.5 acres and 29.3 per cent had between 0.5 and 1.0 acre. Only 4.0 per cent of the households had agricultural landholding more than 2.0 acres. 71.3 per cent of the beneficiary households had agricultural landholding less than one acre.

Of all the households in the lowest income bracket (less than Rs. 10,000 p.a.), which constituted 3.3 per cent of all beneficiary households, 38.5 per cent were landless. Most of the beneficiary households (39.3 per cent) were in the income bracket between Rs. 20,000 and Rs. 32,000 and 15.3 per cent of them were landless. Of the second largest class beneficiary (25.3 per cent) in the income bracket between Rs. 10,000 and Rs. 20,000 p.a., 26.4 per cent were landless. Thus, most of the landless households (13.2 per cent of total beneficiary households) were reportedly in income bracket between Rs. 10,000 and Rs. 32,000 (71.7 per cent of the households within landless category). In the lowest household income category (up to Rs.10,000.), there was none with agricultural landholding above 1.5 acres excepting one. Most of the households as beneficiaries under housing programme had agricultural land less than 2.0 acres. High income and high agricultural landholding moved parallel.

The ownership of productive animals by households shows 50.3 per cent of the households owning cow, 23.8 per cent owning buffalo, 37.8 per cent owning ox, 9.5 per cent owning calf; very few households owning other types of domestic animals like goat, hen, sheep, donkey, horse and rabbit.

Excepting TV owned by 12.0 per cent of the beneficiary households, other durable consumer/producer goods like fridge, motorcycle, sewing machine, mobile phone, almirah, car, washing machine, dressing table and fodder cutting machine were owned by very few households on the hills (Table 3.9).

3.5 Migration and Income of Migrated Persons

8.7 per cent of the sample households used to migrate and the households that got income support from such migration was 7.0 per cent. Thus, 80.0 per cent of the migrated households really got financial help from migration. 69.8 per cent of the migrated households provided financial help to households.

Monthly income following migration stood at Rs. 1,68,700 for the whole population that came to be Rs. 3,183. per capita. Average monthly financial support provided came to be Rs. 825 per capita (Table 3.10).

Table 3.9 : Ownership of Durable Consumer Goods and Producer Goods by Households

Goods	*Total Assets*	*HHs. owned*	*% of HHs. who owned**	*Per HHs. (owned)*	*Per HHs. (sample)*
Refrigerator	11	11	2.8	1	0.03
Motor Bike	11	11	2.8	1	0.03
Television	53	48	12.0	1	0.13
Sewing Machine	4	4	1.0	1	0.01
Loom	2	2	0.5	1	0.01
VCD/DVD	9	9	2.3	1	0.02
Almirah	13	13	3.3	1	0.03
Mobile Phone	10	9	2.3	1	0.03
LPG	8	8	2.0	1	0.02
Plough	10	9	2.3	1	0.03
Car	1	1	0.3	1	0.00
Washing Machine	1	1	0.3	1	0.00
Furniture	2	2	0.6	1	0.00
DTH/ Dish TV	2	2	0.5	1	0.01
Dressing Table	1	1	0.3	1	0.00
Fodder cutting machine	1	1	0.3	1	0.00
Music system	2	2	0.5	1	0.01

Note : * % calculated to total sample.
Source : Field Survey, 2008.

Table 3.10 : Monthly Income (Rs.) of Migrated Persons by Districts and Castes

Districts	*Castes*	*Monthly Income (whole population)*	*Average Monthly Income (PCI)*	*Monthly Support (per Household)*	*Average Monthly Support (Per Capita)*
Pithoragarh	SC	3700	1850	2000	2000
	ST	15000	5000	2000	2000
	General	47000	3133	10500	955
	Total	**65700**	**3285**	**14500**	**1115**
Almora	SC	64000	3765	5733	382
	General	29500	2269	5300	883
	Total	**93500**	**3117**	**11033**	**525**
Chamoli	SC	5000	5000	3000	3000
	General	4500	2250	2000	1000
	Total	9500	3167	5000	1667
Total	SC	72700	3635	10733	631
	ST	15000	5000	2000	2000
	General	81000	2700	17800	937
	Total	**168700**	**3183**	**30533**	**825**

Source : Field Survey, 2008.

3.6 Borrowing by Beneficiary Households by Sources and Sum

70.8 per cent of the beneficiary households did not borrow money during 2004-07. The major sources of borrowing for the households were neighbours, money-lenders, banks and relatives (Table 3.11).

Table 3.11: Sources of Loans Taken by Households

Sources	*Total*	
	No.	*%*
Villagers	35	29.9
Kisan Credit Card	3	2.6
Money Lenders	24	20.5
Banks	34	29.1
Cooperatives	11	9.4
Relatives	23	19.7
No Response	2	1.7
Total	117	100.0

Source : Field Survey, 2008.

Of all the households who borrowed money (29.3 per cent), 35.9 per cent borrowed between Rs. 20,000 and Rs. 40,000 one-quarter borrowed between Rs. 10,000 and Rs. 20,000 one-sixth of the households borrowed more than Rs. 60,000 (Table 3.12).

Table 3.12 : Households by Loan Brackets

Loan Brackets (Rs.)		*Pithoragarh*	*Almora*	*Uttarkashi*	*Chamoli*	*Total*
Up to 10,000	No.	5	3	3	3	14
	%	21.7	12.0	5.3	25.0	12.0
10,000 to 20,000	No.	9	9	10	2	30
	%	39.1	36.0	17.5	16.7	25.6
20,000 to 40,000	No.	7	8	23	4	42
	%	30.4	32.0	40.4	33.3	35.9
40,000 to 60,000	No.	1	1	8	1	11
	%	4.3	4.0	14.0	8.3	9.4
Above 60,000	No.	1	4	13	2	20
	%	4.3	16.0	22.8	16.7	17.1
Total Households	**No.**	**23**	**25**	**57**	**12**	**117**
Taking Loan	**%**	**100.0**	**100.0**	**100.0**	**100.0**	**100.0**

Source : Field Survey, 2008.

3.6.1 *Average Loan, Repayment, Outstanding Loan and Annual Income of Households*

While the average loan taken stood at Rs. 39,774 per household by all castes, loan outstanding remained 87.1 per cent. For the SCs the outstanding loan as percentage of total loan taken stood at 78.3 per cent, for STs 67.1 per cent, for OBCs 89.1 per cent and for General castes 86.7 per cent.

Average repayment as percentage of average borrowing during 2004-07 stood at 44.2 per cent, and outstanding loan stood at 87.1 per cent, implying high interest payment. Each of average borrowing and outstanding loan for all households taken together exceeded the average income per annum of the households, while separately for STs average borrowing and outstanding loan was less than estimated annual income. For income below Rs. 10,000. average borrowing and outstanding loan remained nil. There was no one-to-one correspondence between average borrowing and income bracket, e.g., average borrowing for income bracket Rs. 32,000 to Rs. 50,000 per annum stood at Rs. 27,667.00 whereas for income bracket Rs. 20,000 to Rs. 32,000.00, the average borrowing stood at Rs. 43981. We found different levels of borrowing with respect to average annual income, and loan outstanding correspond to different income brackets and found no specific relation between average income and loans taken (Table 3.13).

3.6.2 *Reasons for Borrowing by Households*

Of those beneficiary households who borrowed money, construction of house was the major reason for borrowing, followed by purchase of animals, cultivation, health, marriage, festivals, and business. (Flow Chart 3.2)

3.7 Housing Condition of Beneficiary Households

37.5 per cent of the beneficiary households had residential

Table 3.13 : Average Loan, Repayment, Loan Outstanding and Average Annual Income

Income Bracket Per Annum (Rs.)	*Castes*	*Average Loan (Rs.)*	*Average Paid (Rs.)*	*Average Outstanding Loan (Rs.)*	*Average Annual Income (Rs.)*
Up to 10000	SC	0	0	0	6800
	OBC	0	0	0	7200
	General	0	0	0	6840
	Total	**0**	**0**	**0**	**6877**
10,000 to 20,000	SC	26800	9350	25113	15432
	ST	25000	5000	20000	15600
	OBC	50714	20000	60000	14753
	General	28858	9950	38000	14945
	Total	**34000**	**12385**	**39567**	**15220**
20,000 to 32,000	SC	31808	17156	24818	25147
	ST	40000	16000	20000	25292
	OBC	54688	15643	42500	25096
	General	63125	28600	53500	25180
	Total	**43981**	**17466**	**34904**	**25158**
32,000 to 50,000	SC	24250	23875	13375	39442
	ST	0	0	0	39333
	OBC	37857	15000	30000	37500
	General	21600	4000	20000	38727
	Total	**27667**	**19286**	**20895**	**39023**
50,000 to 75,000	SC	28750	7000	24000	60700
	ST	24000	24000	0	58200
	OBC	200000	0	200000	60000
	General	71000	43333	41400	62300
	Total	**63091**	**25000**	**50300**	**60389**
Above 75,000	SC	0	0	0	150000
	ST	20000	20000	0	96600
	OBC	44000	10000	40000	90000
	General	15000	0	18000	119733
	Total	**26333**	**15000**	**29000**	**113600**
Total	SC	28865	16442	22617	27249
	ST	29800	16200	20000	42921
	OBC	54344	16000	48433	24854
	General	45577	26633	39523	37956
	Total	**39774**	**17568**	**34640**	**31299**

Source : Field Survey, 2008.

area between 200 sq.ft. and 500 sq.ft. while 19.3 per cent had area between 1000 sq.ft. and 2,000 sq.ft. Of the IAY beneficiary households, 43.8 per cent had residential area between 200

Flow Chart 3.2 : Reasons for Borrowing by Households

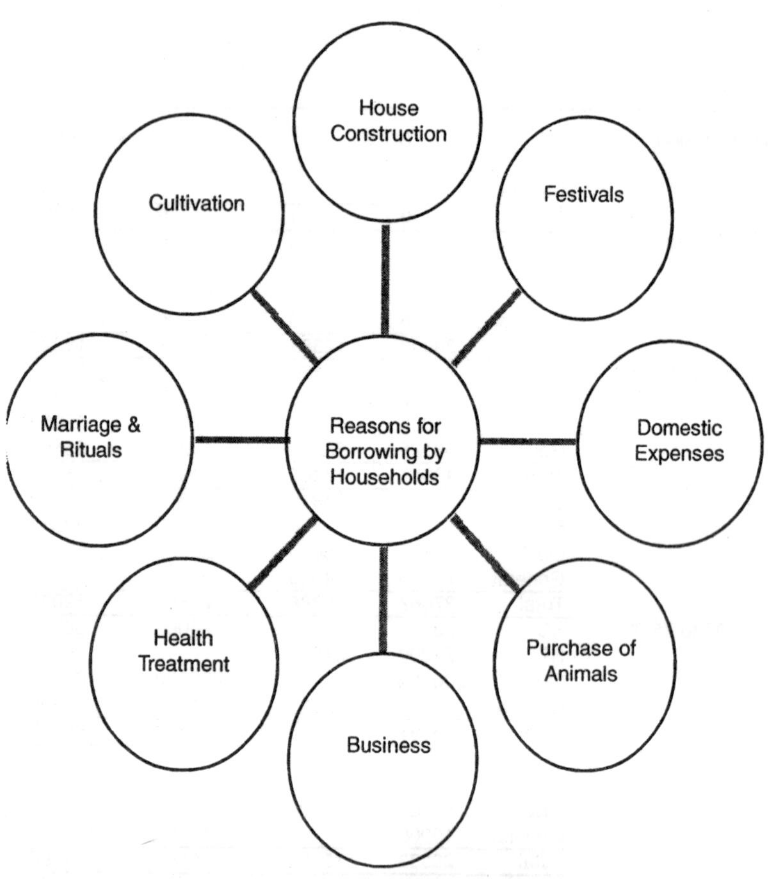

Source : Field Survey, 2008.

and 500 sq.ft. while 16.5 per cent had area between 1,000 sq.ft. and 2000 sq.ft. Of the beneficiary households under CCSRHP, 35.8 per cent had area between 200 and 500 sq.ft. while 27.2 per cent had residential area between 1,000 sq.ft. and 2,000 sq.ft. Most of the beneficiary households under different schemes, thus, had residential area between 200 sq.ft. and 500 sq.ft. in a general scenario of a big range of residential area (Table 3.14).

Table 3.14 : Residential Area of Houses for Households under Housing Programmes

Residential Area (sq. ft.)		*IAY*	*CCSRHP*	*Others*	*Total*
Up to 100	No.	3	0	0	3
	%	1.3	0.0	0.0	0.8
100 to 200	No.	44	12	8	64
	%	19.6	14.8	8.4	16.0
200 to 500	No.	98	29	23	150
	%	43.8	35.8	24.2	37.5
500 to 1000	No.	34	6	25	65
	%	15.2	7.4	26.3	16.3
1000 to 2000	No.	37	22	18	77
	%	16.5	27.2	18.9	19.3
Above 2000	No.	8	12	21	41
	%	3.6	14.8	22.1	10.3
Total	No.	224	81	95	400
	%	100.0	100.0	100.0	100.0

Source : Field Survey, 2008.

3.7.1 Residential Area by Income Per Annum of Households

Of all the households having residential area between 200 and 500 sq.ft., 41.3 per cent had annual income between Rs. 20,000 and Rs. 32,000 Of all the beneficiary households with residential area between 1,000 and 2,000 sq.ft., 36.4 per cent had income between Rs. 20,000 and Rs. 32,000 Of all the households with residential area more than 2,000 sq.ft., 43.9 per cent had income between Rs. 20,000 and Rs. 32,000.00. Of all the households with residential area between 100 and 200 sq.ft., 40.6 per cent were in income bracket between Rs. 20,000 and Rs. 32,000 It seems the households in the income bracket between Rs. 20,000 and Rs. 32,000 dominated in the process of being selected and built residence by varying areas (Table 3.15).

Table 3.15 : Distribution of Residential Area (in sq. ft.) by Household Income per Annum

Income per annum (Rs.) \ Residential Area (sq. ft.)		Up to 100	100 to 200	200 to 500	500 to 1000	1000 to 2000	More than 2000	Total
Up to 10000	No.	0	0	6	4	2	1	13
	%	0.0	0.0	4.0	6.2	2.6	2.4	3.3
10000 to 20000	No.	2	22	37	12	14	14	101
	%	66.7	34.4	24.7	18.5	18.2	34.1	25.3
20000 to 32000	No.	1	26	62	22	28	18	157
	%	33.3	40.6	41.3	33.8	36.4	43.9	39.3
32000 to 50000	No.	0	10	29	18	16	4	77
	%	0.0	15.6	19.3	27.7	20.8	9.8	19.3
50000 to 75000	No.	0	3	14	5	13	2	37
	%	0.0	4.7	9.3	7.7	16.9	4.9	9.3
Above 75000	No.	0	3	2	4	4	2	15
	%	0.0	4.7	1.3	6.2	5.2	4.9	3.8
Total	**No.**	**3**	**64**	**150**	**65**	**77**	**41**	**400**
	%	**100.0**	**100.0**	**100.0**	**100.0**	**100.0**	**100.0**	**100.0**

Source : Field Survey, 2008.

Per capita residential area over all the districts for all categories of households was 140 sq.ft. (Table 3.16).

Table 3.16 : Per Household and Per Capita Residential Area

(Area in sq.ft.)

Districts	Per Household Area			Per Capita Area		
	Residential	Constructed	Constructed Under Programme	Residential	Constructed	Constructed Under Programme
Pithoragarh	217	85	67	41	16	13
Almora	132	86	66	25	16	13
Uttarkashi	224	84	73	43	16	14
Chamoli	160	79	61	31	15	12
Total	**733**	**334**	**267**	**140**	**64**	**51**

Source : Field Survey, 2008.

Total constructed area was 45.6 per cent of total residential area, covering all districts and households by castes. Total constructed area is the summation of *pucca* area, semi-*pucca* area and *kutcha* area. For all households covering all districts, *pucca* area as percentage of constructed area was 75.8 that was 20.9 for semi-*pucca* and 3.4 for *kutcha* houses. In case of each district and by caste, *pucca* area as percentage of total constructed area had the lead followed by semi-*pucca* area and then *kutcha* area (Table 3.17).

Table 3.17 : Constructed Area in Houses of Households by Districts

(Area in sq.ft.)

Districts	*Per Household*			*Per Capita*		
	Residential Area	*Total Constructed Area*	*Constructed Area Under Programme*	*Residential Area*	*Total Constructed Area*	*Constructed Area Under Programme*
Pithoragarh	217	85	67	41	16	13
Almora	132	86	66	25	16	13
Uttarkashi	224	84	73	43	16	14
Chamoli	160	79	61	31	15	12
Total	**733**	**334**	**267**	**140**	**64**	**51**

Source : Field Survey, 2008.

3.7.2 Availability of Rooms by Types of Construction and Area

Of all the beneficiary households, 15.5 per cent had no *pucca* rooms, 74.8 per cent had no semi-*pucca* rooms and 90.5 per cent had no *kutcha* rooms. 40.3 per cent of the beneficiary households had two *pucca* rooms while the percentage of households having number of *pucca* rooms more than two was very low covering all the households.

Of all the beneficiary households, 65.5 per cent had only *pucca* rooms and 13.0 per cent had only semi-*pucca* rooms. Only 0.8 per cent had *kutcha* rooms. Households occupied also rooms of mixed nature, like 10.8 per cent occupying both *pucca* and semi-*pucca* rooms, 7.3 per cent occupying both *pucca* and *kutcha* rooms, 2.5 per cent occupying both semi-*pucca* and *kutcha* rooms and 0.3 per cent occupying all types of rooms, *pucca*, semi-*pucca* and *kutcha*.

3.8 Housing Problems in Existence

The problems visualized by Panchayat representatives in housing included non-suitability of houses in different seasons in the hilly region, non-ownership of land, landslide and earthquake, big family size and hence inadequate number of rooms, division of household and requirement for more houses, non-availability of construction materials, and vibration of constructed houses because of stone blasting.

3.9 Types, Uses and Ownership of Houses

Of all the houses under housing programme, 55.8 per cent were traditional, 38.8 per cent modern and 5.5 per cent a mix of both. Of all the SC beneficiary households, 57.6 per cent houses were traditional and 42.0 per cent modern. The respective percentages for STs were 34.9 and 32.6 while for OBCs these were 78.8 and 15.4. For households in general castes, these houses by types were 49.0 per cent in traditional type and 47.0 per cent in modern type (Table 3.18).

Table 3.18 : Types of Houses by Castes

Types		*SC*	*ST*	*OBC*	*General*	*Total*
Traditional	No.	118	15	41	49	223
	%	57.6	34.9	78.8	49.0	55.8
Modern	No.	86	14	8	47	155
	%	42.0	32.6	15.4	47.0	38.8
Both	No.	1	14	3	4	22
	%	0.5	32.6	5.8	4.0	5.5
Total	**No.**	**205**	**43**	**52**	**100**	**400**
	%	**100.0**	**100.0**	**100.0**	**100.0**	**100.0**

Source : Field Survey, 2008.

Of all the *pucca* houses, 94.4 per cent were only residential, the rest for residence-*cum*-shops and residence-*cum*-animal shed. Of all semi-*pucca* houses, 63.9 per cent were only for residence, while 27.8 per cent were for residence-*cum*-animal shed, and the rest for animal shed only (7.2 per cent) and for residence-*cum*-shops (1.0 per cent). Of all *kutcha* houses, 41.7 per cent were for residential purposes, 38.9 per cent for animal shed, 8.3 per cent for residence-*cum*-animal shed and 11.1 per cent for kitchen. There were district-wise variations in the type of houses used by purposes (Table 3.19).

Table 3.19 : Uses of Houses by Types by Districts

Types	*Uses*	*Pithoragarh*		*Almora*		*Uttarkashi*		*Chamoli*		*Total*	
		No.	%	No.	%	No.	%	No.	%	No.	%
Pucca	Residential	90	98.9	73	86.9	71	97.3	88	94.6	322	94.4
	Residence-cum-Shops	1	1.1	1	1.2	0	0.0	1	1.1	3	0.9
	Residence-cum-Animal shed	0	0.0	10	11.9	2	2.7	4	4.3	16	4.7
	Total	**91**	**100.0**	**84**	**100.0**	**73**	**100.0**	**93**	**100.0**	**341**	**100.0**
Semi *Pucca*	Residential	11	61.1	13	56.5	20	64.5	18	72.0	62	63.9
	Animal Shed	4	22.2	0	0.0	0	0.0	3	12.0	7	7.2
	Residence-cum-Shops	0	0.0	1	4.3	0	0.0	0	0.0	1	1.0
	Residence cum Animal shed	3	16.7	9	39.1	11	35.5	4	16.0	27	27.8
	Total	**18**	**100.0**	**23**	**100.0**	**31**	**100.0**	**25**	**100.0**	**97**	**100.0**
Kutcha	Residential	7	46.7	0	0.0	7	77.8	1	11.1	15	41.7
	Kitchen	3	20.0	0	0.0	0	0.0	1	11.1	4	11.1
	Animal shed	4	26.7	2	66.7	2	22.2	6	66.7	14	38.9
	Residence-*cum*-Animal shed	1	6.7	1	33.3	0	0.0	1	11.1	3	8.3
	Total	**15**	**100.0**	**3**	**100.0**	**9**	**100.0**	**9**	**100.0**	**36**	**100.0**

Source : Field Survey, 2008.

Of all the houses occupied by households, 80 per cent was for residential purposes and 16.3 per cent for cottage industries-cum-residence. 3 per cent had houses for shop-cum-residential purposes and 0.8 per cent had house only for shops. 98.8 per cent of the households had ownership over residential house. Thus, rented houses and houses owned by others were negligible.

3.10 Availability of Basic Facilities in Houses

Of all the houses of the beneficiary households, 63.5 per cent had toilet inside the house, 56. per cent had kitchen, 71.8 per cent had drainage and 93.3 per cent had open space. 82.6 per cent of the households who had drainage in their houses had open drainage. Only 4.5 per cent had covered drainage and 12.9 per cent had unplanned drainage.

73.5 per cent of the households had electricity as a source of light in houses. Most of the households depended on kerosene in absence of electricity. The uses of solar light, battery system were negligible.

58.0 per cent of the households used tap water for drinking purposes; 26.8 per cent used natural waterfall/ spring and 10.5 per cent used narrow water stream/drain water for drinking purposes. Handpump as a source of drinking water was negligible (Flow Chart 3.3).

Flow Chart 3.3 : Sources of Drinking Water for Households

Tap Water

River

Sources of Drinking Water for Households

Natural Waterfall/ Spring

Nerrow Water Stream Drain

Handpump

Source : Field Survey, 2008.

18.5 per cent of the households had sources of drinking water inside house, 19.5 per cent had sources within 25 meter from the house. For 15.2 per cent of the houses, sources of drinking water were between 25 and 50 metres. For 13.5 per cent of the households, the source remained beyond half a km. Of the households using tap water, 31.9 per cent had it inside the house, and 42.7 per cent had it at a distance less than 50 meters. The distance of sources of drinking water varied depending on the source; in case of tap water the distance was generally less while in case of natural waterfall/ spring the distance was generally more.

3.11 Types of Fuel Used by Households

99.0 per cent of the households used wood as fuel. 37.8 per cent used leaves and straw as fuel, 18.8 per cent used LPG, 12.8 per cent used cow dung cake and only 0.5 per cent used kerosene. In case of all the districts excepting Pithoragarh, use of wood was cent per cent for households. Of those using types of fuel in Pithoragah, use of LPG was significant (for 42.0 per cent of the households) while wood remained the major fuel (96.0 per cent of the households). Use of cow dung cake was used most as fuel in Uttarkashi (26.0 per cent of households reporting) which was much less for other districts. Use of leaves and straw was significant in Uttarkashi and Chamoli. Thus, the households depended on a number of alternative uses of fuel with wood ranked first.

3.12 Double Settlement of Households in Hill Region

Of all the beneficiary households, 11.5 per cent had double settlement. 88.5 per cent were settled in the single house throughout the year, which was 100 per cent in Almora. The least settled in the single house were the households in

Chamoli, where 32 per cent had double settlement. It was mainly the STs who used to move out, that is, had double settlement.

3.12.1 Reasons for Double Settlement

The major reasons for double settlement were snowfall and cultivation. For STs snowfall explained relocation for 91.2 per cent of those households, while for SCs cultivation explained relocation of 83.3 per cent of these households. For OBCs, cultivation explained the whole of relocation.

Of all those households who had double settlement (11.5 per cent), 65.2 per cent moved out with whole family while 34.8 per cent moved out with some members of the family. For ST households, 79.4 per cent of the households moved out with whole family, which was 16.7 per cent in case of SC households. The average period of staying in the second settlement varied between five and six months.

The moving out occurred mostly (50.0 per cent of all migrants) from the peak of the hills, while 28.3 per cent moved out from the middle of the hills and 21.7 per cent from valley. Thus, the higher the altitude by first settlement, the higher was the occurrence of moving out for second settlement. In case of Pithoragarh and Uttarkashi, it was 'moving out' only from the peak of the hills. In case of Chamoli, it was also from middle part and valley. In case of Almora, no report of moving out from the sample households was received. The average distance by which the second settlement was reached was 58 km. that was 45 km. from top of hill, 70 km. from middle of the hill and 72 km. from valley.

3.12.2 Types of Houses and Ownership at Relocation

Of all the households who had double settlement, the second house was *pucca* for 39.1 per cent, *kutcha* for 6.5 per cent, tent for 8.7 per cent and cottage for 6.5 per cent. Of the migrants, 69.8 per cent owned the second house, while others used to stay in houses of relatives, government and friends. The *pucca* second house was only self-owned. The same was true for *kutcha* second house. The nature of the second house and ownership of the second house thus varied. However, in most cases it was self-owned.

3.12.3 Occupations and Average Income of Moved-out Households

Of all the migrant households, 34.8 per cent migrated for cultivation and earned income from the second settlement to the extent of Rs. 1,563. per household p.m. Another 34.8 per cent migrated for labour (wage work) and earned Rs. 1,469 p.m. per household. For weaving/sewing, 23.9 per cent moved out to earn Rs. 1,442 per household p.m. There were few others who moved out for animal husbandry and business.

3.12.4 Location of Moved-out Place and Problems

In the second location by settlement for the migrant households, the major problems faced were availability of water and electricity (47.8 per cent reporting), followed by less employment opportunity and difficulty in getting food-grains from FPSs. 26.1 per cent of the migrants reported 'no problems' in second settlement. The problems regarding water and electricity were mentioned most in case of second settlement on top of hills, where half of the migrants used to get re-settled for a temporary period of five to six months per year. The other half used to re-settle on middle of hills and valley. 'No problems' were reported more in case of re-settlement on the middle of the hill and valley (Table 3.20).

Table 3.20 : Location of Moved-out Place and Problems faced by Households

Problems	*Top of Hill*		*Middle of Hill*		*Valley*		*Total*	
	No.	*%*	*No.*	*%*	*No.*	*%*	*No.*	*%*
Very less Employment Opportunity	0	0.0	1	7.7	2	20.0	3	6.5
Difficulty to getting Food - grains from FPSs	0	0.0	0	0.0	1	10.0	1	2.2
Non-availability of Water and Electricity	15	65.2	5	38.5	2	20.0	22	47.8
Difficulty to getting Foodgrains from FPSs + Water and Electricity Problems	0	0.0	0	0.0	1	10.0	1	2.2
Water and Electricity + Very less Employment Opportunity	7	30.4	0	0.0	0	0.0	7	15.2
No Problems	1	4.3	7	53.8	4	40.0	12	26.1
Total	23	100.0	13	100.0	10	100.0	46	100.0

Note : The education of children is not affected during the period of migration because of the facility available at both the places.

Source : Field Survey, 2008.

4

Impact of Housing Programmes on Households

In order to assess the impact of rural housing programmes on households, we covered 400 households from 54 villages from the selected districts of Uttarakhand. We assessed impact on the beneficiary households by their eligibility, methods of selection, location of newly constructed house, number of rooms and area constructed under the housing programmes, materials used for construction of houses, cost of construction, construction of toilet and its use, installation of smokeless stove, mode of payment and support under the programme, safety and security of households in newly constructed house, protection of households against seasonal and natural calamities, impact of housing by indicators like self-respect of individuals and family peace, and linkage of housing programme with other development programmes. We have analyzed all these aspects in this chapter.

4.1 Households Selected under Housing Programmes by Priority Categories

The households selected under housing programmes followed the priority categories like being in SC and ST, households affected by natural calamities, physically and mentally challenged persons, widows and unmarried women from SC/ST households, widows of personnel from defence, etc. (Table 4.1).

Table 4.1: Households Selected for Housing under Priority Categories by Districts

Categories	*Pithora-garh*	*Almora*	*Uttar-kashi*	*Chamoli*	*Total*	*As % of total*
SC/ST Households, Headed by widows and unmarried women	6	5	3	1	15	3.8
SC/ST Households effected by flood & natural calamities like earthquake, cyclone	5	1	9	20	35	8.8
Other SC/ST Households	51	53	34	39	177	44.3
Families/widows of personnel from defense services/ paramilitary forces, killed in service	1	0	0	0	1	0.3
Non-SC/ST Households	11	16	37	20	84	21.0
Physically and Mentally challenged persons	0	1	0	0	1	0.3
APL Households with annual income at the margin of Rs. 32,000.	26	24	17	20	87	21.8
Total	**100**	**100**	**100**	**100**	**400**	**100.0**

Source : Field Survey, 2008.

The selection of households under priority categories followed the similar pattern of inclusion for the programme like Indira Awaas Yojana. For credit-cum-subsidy scheme (CCS) it was only APL households with annual income at the margin of Rs. 32,000 that derived the housing benefits. For other housing programmes, the selection criteria are based on Scheduled Castes/Scheduled Tribes households, and protection against natural calamities (Table 4.2).

4.2 Selection of Beneficiary Households : Positive and Normative Methods

Panchayats took the lead in selecting households under

Table 4.2 : Households Selected for Housing under Priority Categories by Programmes

Categories		*IAY*	*CCSRHP*	*Others*	*Total*
SC/ST Households, headed by widows and unmarried women	No.	15	0	0	15
	%	6.7	0.0	0.0	3.8
SC/ST Households affected by natural calamities (like flood, earthquake, cyclone) and man-made calamities like riot	No.	6	0	29	35
	%	2.7	0.0	30.5	8.8
Other SC/ST Households	No.	147	0	30	177
	%	65.6	0.0	31.6	44.3
Families/widows of personnel from defense services/paramilitary forces, killed in war	No.	1	0	0	1
	%	0.4	0.0	0.0	0.3
Non-SC/ST Households	No.	49	0	35	84
	%	21.9	0.0	36.8	21.0
Physically and Mentally Challenged Persons	No.	1	0	0	1
	%	0.4	0.0	0.0	0.3
APL Households with annual income at the margin of Rs. 32,000.00	No.	5	81	1	87
	%	2.2	100.0	1.1	21.8
Total	No.	224	81	95	400
	%	100.0	100.0	100.0	100.0

Source : Field Survey, 2008.

housing schemes. Of total households, Panchayats selected 71.7 per cent, block officials 13.5 per cent, Gram Pradhans 10.2 per cent and others like Block Development Officers, relatives, local powerful persons and mediators selected the rest. In case of IAY, 79.5 per cent were selected by Panchayats; while 51.9 per cent of the households under Credit-cum-Subsidy Rural Housing Policy were selected by Panchayats. Thus, Panchayats played a significant role in selecting households as beneficiaries.

In case the households were selected by Panchayats and/or Gram Pradhans, 64.0 per cent were selected through open meetings of Gram Sabha, 31.1 per cent through eligibility, and the rest through block officials, personal approach, caste base and local powerful persons. The other major method was following permanent wait list. In addition, the BPL list and the poor housing condition also guided the selection.

Under Indira Awaas Yojana, 72.5 per cent were through open meetings of Gram Sabha, which was 90.5 per cent under Credit-cum-Subsidy Rural Housing Policy and 64.2 per cent in case of other housing programmes. By eligibility criterion under Indira Awaas Yojana, Panchayats determined 27.5 per cent and Gram Pradhans determined 84.6 per cent. In case of Credit-cum-Subsidy Rural Housing Policy, Pradhans had no role. The criteria adopted by Gram Panchayats and Pradhans in selecting households were different.

As opined by the Panchayat representatives, the major method for selection of beneficiaries should be through open meetings of Gram Panchayat, BPL list, and wait list in Indira Awaas Yojana. The other criteria opined were ownership over land for construction of house, widowhood, and physically challenged persons (Box 4.1).

Box 4.1: Methods Adopted for Selection of Beneficiary Households (Reported by Gram Panchayats)

Positive Methods	*Normative Methods*
• *Open Meetings of Gram Sabha* • *BPL List* • *Permanent Wait List* • *Having Land for Construction of House* • *Poor Housing Condition*	• *Based on open meetings of Gram Sabha* • *Should be a BPL household* • *Having land for construction of house* • *Poor condition of house* • *Widow or Handicapped person* • *Based on wait list* • *Beneficiary selected by block office*

Source : Field Survey, 2008.

Most of the beneficiary households reported that needy households were selected by Panchayats. The major difficulties in selection of beneficiary households under housing programme were old and obsolete wait list, provision of reservation preventing selection of deserving candidates, difficulties in rejecting deserving households in the open meetings.

The reasons for exclusion of eligible households were limited number of target houses for the Gram Panchayat, adverse reporting by implementing body, names missing in BPL list, Pradhan and block officials opposing the selection. Ignorance was a major factor for exclusion of eligible households.

4.3 Selection of Location for Construction of Houses

Ninty per cent of the beneficiary households selected their own location for construction of houses. This was 99.1 per cent under Indira Awaas Yojana, 98.8 per cent under CCSRHP, and 98.9 per cent for others.

Twentiy eight per cent of the households located their houses on the peak of the hills while 56.0 per cent had location on middle part of the hills and 16.0 per cent on the valley. 31.0 per cent of total houses constructed in Pithoragarh were on peak of the hills. Middle part of the hills was the favoured zone for construction of houses (Table 4.3).

Table 4.3: Location of the Houses of Households on the Hills

Districts	*Peak*	*Middle part of hill*	*Valley*	*Total*
Pithoragarh	31	44	25	100
Almora	28	49	23	100
Uttarkashi	25	62	13	100
Chamoli	28	69	3	100
Total	112	224	64	400
As % of Total	28.0	56.0	16.0	100.0

Source : Field Survey, 2008.

Of the houses located at the peak of the hills, 48.2 per cent were traditional, 42.9 per cent modern and the rest a mix of both. Of the houses built on the middle part of the hills, 57.1 per cent were traditional, 37.5 per cent modern and the rest a mix of both. Of the houses built in the valley, 64.1 per cent were traditional and 35.9 per cent modern.

93.7 per cent of the constructed houses under housing programmes were on own land within main habitation and the rest on own land outside main habitation. Of the IAY houses, these percentages were 95.1 and 4.9 respectively; in case of CCSRHP, these percentages were 96.3 and 3.7 respectively.

4.4 Types of Construction and Uses of Houses

50.3 per cent of the households constructed their new houses in new place while 31.3 per cent constructed after demolition of old house, 17.3 per cent went for repair and renovation of old house, and 0.3 per cent constructed only toilet. Under Indira Awaas Yojana, 45.1 per cent of the households constructed house newly, 33.5 per cent constructed after demolition of old house, 19.6 per cent went for repair of house. In case of houses under Credit-cum-Subsidy Rural Housing Policy, new construction was for 54.3 per cent of the households, while 29.6 per cent constructed after demolition of old house and 14.8 per cent went for repair and renovation of old house (Table 4.4).

Table 4.4 : Types of Construction Done by Households by Programmes

Construction		*IAY*	*CCSRHP*	*Others*	*Total*
Newly constructed on new place	No.	101	44	56	201
	%	45.1	54.3	58.9	50.3
Constructed after demolition of	No.	75	24	26	125
old House	%	33.5	29.6	27.4	31.3
Repairing or renewal of old house	No.	44	12	13	69
	%	19.6	14.8	13.7	17.3
Only Toilet is constructed	No.	1	0	0	1
	%	0.4	0.0	0.0	0.3
No construction	No.	3	1	0	4
	%	1.3	1.2	0.0	1.0
Total	No.	224	81	95	400
	%	100.0	100.0	100.0	100.0

Source : Field Survey, 2008.

92.8 per cent of the newly constructed houses were complete and were in use by the beneficiary households, 1.5 per cent were complete but not in use, 4.3 per cent were under construction, 0.3 per cent had been transferred. Under Indira Awaas Yojana, 91.1 per cent were complete and in use while 4.5 per cent were under construction, 1.8 per cent were complete but not in use and 0.4 per cent were complete and in use while 4.9 per cent were under construction (Flow Chart 4.1).

Flow Chart 4.1: Use of Houses

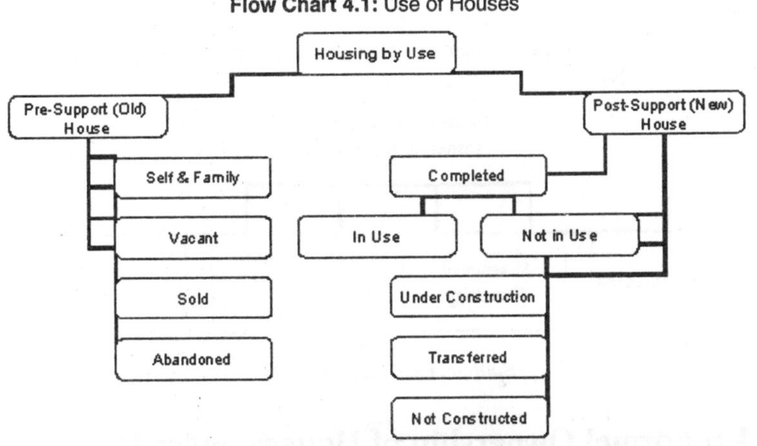

Source : Field Survey, 2008.

4.4.1 Reasons for Non-Completion or Non-Use of Houses

The reasons why complete houses were not being used were inadequate space, absence of required facilities, long distance from village/main habitation and insecure place. The reasons why houses remained under construction or 'yet to be constructed' were shortage of finance, death of family member, and difficulties in making materials available. In case of Credit-cum-Subsidy Rural Housing Policy, the non-use of house after completing construction was absent (Flow Chart 4.2. & 4.3)

Flow Chart 4.2 : Reasons for Non-Completion of Houses

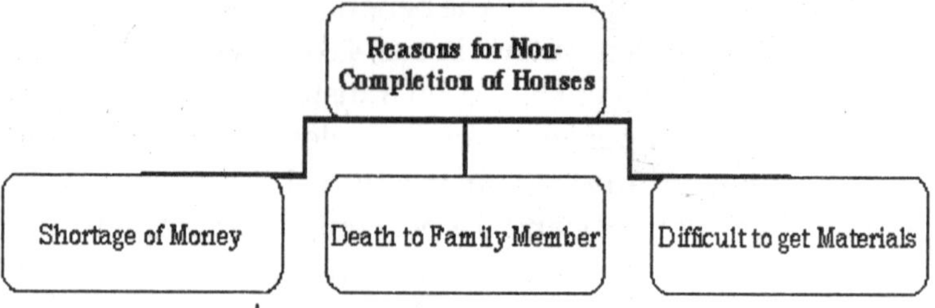

Source : Field Survey, 2008.

Flow Chart 4.3 : Reasons for Non-Use of Constructed Houses

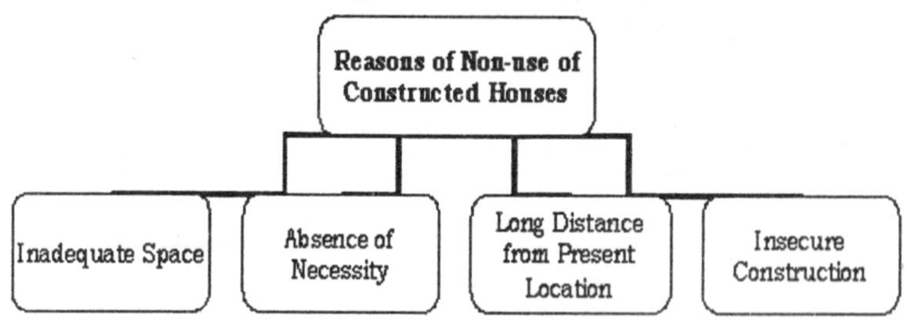

Source : Field Survey, 2008.

4.5 Formal Ownership of Houses under Housing Programmes

55.8 per cent of the houses were formally owned by wife of the (male) head of the household and 40.3 per cent ownership was maintained by the male head (husband) of the household. Of the Indira Awaas Yojana beneficiaries, 64.3 per cent of ownership of houses was maintained by the wife (female) of the head of the household and 30.4 per cent by the male (husband or head) of the household. In case of CCSRHP, the ownership went to male head by 86.4 per cent while 9.9 per cent went to wife (female) of household. Very few houses were owned by other members of the household (Table 4.5).

Table 4.5 : Formal Ownership of Houses under Housing Programmes

Ownership		*IAY*	*CCSRHP*	*Others*	*Total*
Wife of Head	No.	144	8	71	223
of the Household	%	64.3	9.9	74.7	55.8
Husband or Head	No.	68	70	23	161
of the Household	%	30.4	86.4	24.2	40.3
Other Male	No.	5	3	1	9
member of family	%	2.2	3.7	1.1	2.3
Other Female	No.	7	0	0	7
member of family	%	3.1	0.0	0.0	1.8
Total	No.	224	81	95	400
	%	100.0	100.0	100.0	100.0

Source : Field Survey, 2008.

4.6 Constructed Area of Houses under Housing Programmes

Households under IAY constructed houses by areas ranging from less than 150 sq.ft. to more than 500 sq.ft. Most of the houses (69.1 per cent) constructed under CCSRHP were in the range of area between 225 sq.ft. and 500 sq.ft. Overall, covering all schemes, around 50.0 per cent of the houses were in the range between 225 sq. ft. and 500 sq. ft. by area.

Pucca construction as percentage of constructed area for Indira Awaas Yojana houses was 74.2 while semi-*pucca* construction as percentage of constructed area was 22.3 and *kutcha* construction as percentage of constructed area 3.5. Total constructed area as percentage of total residential area was 57.8 under Indira Awaas Yojana, which was 52.2 in case of Credit-cum-Subsidy Rural Housing Policy and 26.8 in case of other housing schemes. Overall, constructed area as percentage of total residential area was 45.6 covering all schemes. Under Credit-cum-Subsidy Rural Housing Policy, *pucca* construction as percentage of constructed area was 83.3, semi-*pucca* 12.7 and *kutcha* 4.0. The same pattern holds good in case of houses constructed under other schemes (Table 4.6).

Table 4.6 : Average Residential and Construction Area by Housing Programmes
(*Area in sq.ft.*)

Particulars	*IAY*	*CCSRHP*	*Others*	*Total*
Constructed under Programme	260	343	231	270
As % of constructed area	82.9	77.2	79.5	80.7
Pucca Construction	232	370	203	253
As % of constructed area	74.2	83.3	70.1	75.8
Semi *Pucca* Construction	70	56	81	70
As % of constructed area	22.3	12.7	27.9	20.9
Kutcha Construction	11	18	6	11
As % of constructed area	3.5	4.0	2.1	3.4
Total Construction Area	313	445	290	334
As % of Total Residential area	57.8	52.2	26.8	45.6
Total Residential Area	542	852	1084	733

Source : Field Survey, 2008.

For all the districts, on average, *pucca* construction as percentage of total constructed area was 75.8; semi-*pucca* construction 20.9 and *kutcha* construction 3.4.

4.6.1 Construction of Houses by Selected Parameters under Housing Programmes

Thus, 90.0 per cent of the houses were constructed within one year period. Under Indira Awaas Yojana, 89.3 per cent of the houses were constructed within one year, which under Credit-cum-Subsidy Rural Housing Policy came to be 93.9 per cent. In case of houses under other schemes, 88.3 per cent were constructed within one year.

88.4 per cent of the houses at the peak were constructed within one year, the percentage being 91.0 for houses constructed on the middle part of the hills and 89.1 per cent at the valley. No construction of house under the programme took more than one year to construct in the valley. More than 80.0 per cent of the houses were constructed by six months on the middle part of the hills and valley, while around 70.0 per cent were constructed by six months on the top.

The duration of construction on average at the peak of the hills was 7.1 months, which came down to 5.3 months in the middle of the hills and 3.7 months at the valley, implying more time required constructing a house on higher altitude. Of the households who reported the period of construction, 28.5 per cent constructed at the peak, 56.5 per cent on the middle part and 15.0 per cent in the valley.

Of the total houses constructed under IAY, 57.1 per cent constructed two rooms, and 29.0 per cent constructed one room, and 11.6 per cent constructed three rooms and above. Of the total houses constructed under CCSRHP, 49.4 per cent households constructed two rooms, 24.7 per cent constructed three rooms and 19.8 per cent four rooms and above. In case of houses constructed under other schemes, 72.6 per cent constructed two rooms. Overall, 59.3 per cent of all households constructed two rooms that were mainly in houses having area between 150 and 215 sq.ft. and between 225 and 300 sq.ft. The households having one room had area of house less than 150 sq.ft. The households having three rooms had houses with area between 300 and 500 sq.ft. and the households by having four rooms had houses with area above 500 sq.ft. Thus, in general, number of more rooms in houses was associated with higher area of the house.

49.3 per cent of the households constructed houses by self-supervision and hired labour, while 48.8 per cent provided family labour and supervised construction work. The catalysts responsible for construction work were, thus, the individual and family labour. Even in case of houses constructed under Credit-cum-Subsidy Rural Housing Policy, it was mainly self and family labour. The role of contractors in construction was least in all the schemes (Flow Chart 4.4).

Flow Chart 4.4 : Houses Constructed by Persons under Housing Programmes

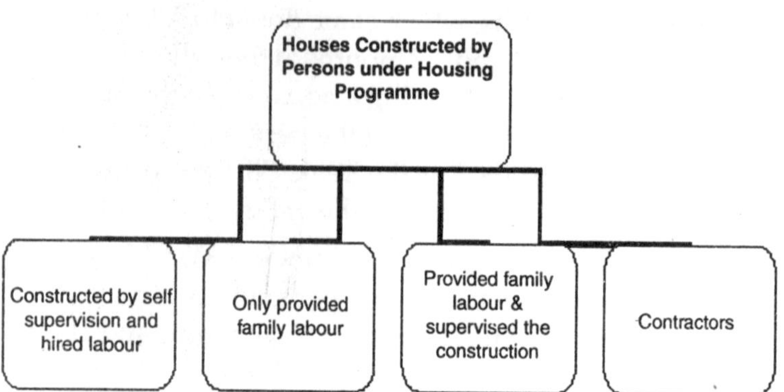

Source : Field Survey, 2008.

4.6.2 Materials Used for Construction of Houses

In construction of floor of the house, 57.3 per cent used cement with stone and stone chips (to make it *pucca*). There were also two (multi) storey houses where ground floor was soil-made and upper floor wood-made (8.0 per cent).

Under IAY, 50.4 per cent cemented their floor with use of stone and stone chips and 37.1 per cent maintained soil floor, the percentages being 67.9 and 21.0 in case of Credit-cum-Subsidy Rural Housing Policy. In case of floor in houses under other schemes, the same pattern was followed. In case of Indira Awaas Yojana, 6.7 per cent of the households had soil floor as 'ground floor' and wood floor as upper floor, which was 9.9 per cent under Credit-cum-Subsidy Rural Housing Policy and 9.5 per cent in case of other schemes.

For construction of walls in houses under housing programme, 33.3 per cent used stone and soil, while 44.8 per cent used stone and cement, 9.8 per cent used brick and cement, 1.8 per cent stone and wood, 4.5 per cent only stone, 3.8 per cent used cemented blocks and cement.

Thus, households chose different types of wall for safety-cum-durability and to fulfil season-specific requirements.

Of the houses constructed under Indira Awaas Yojana, 42.0 per cent constructed wall with stone and cement while 37.1 per cent constructed with stone and soil, 9.4 per cent constructed wall with brick and cement, 3.6 per cent constructed with only stone, 2.2 per cent stone and wood. In use of wall constructed in houses under Credit-cum-Subsidy Rural Housing Policy, 48.1 per cent made it with stone and cement while 34.6 per cent with stone and soil. The use of stone and wood, only stone, cemented blocks and cement were also used for construction of wall under Credit-cum-Subsidy Rural Housing Policy. For houses under other schemes, the major materials for construction of wall were stone and cement, stone and soil, brick and cement.

Of all the roofs constructed in houses under the housing programme, 78.0 per cent of the households had RCC roof, followed by 16.0 per cent iron sheets and wood. In case of 61.3 per cent of the beneficiary households, the materials used for construction of roof in houses under housing programme was RCC. 19.5 per cent households had roof made of iron sheets and wood, while 6.5 per cent had it made of slate and wood. Only stone sheet (for 6.3 per cent of the households) and Sarpet (all types of leaf) were also used to construct roof. Under Indira Awaas Yojana, RCC roof covered 59.8 per cent of the households and iron sheets and wood made roof covered 19.6 per cent of households. Slate and wood covered 8.0 per cent of the households. In case of Indira Awaas Yojana, 4.5 per cent of the households were still in the process of building roof. In case of roof in houses under Credit-cum-Subsidy Rural Housing Policy, RCC covered 69.1 per cent of the households and Iron sheets and wood covered 21.1 per cent of households (Flow Chart 4.5).

Flow Chart 4.5 : Materials Used for Construction of Houses

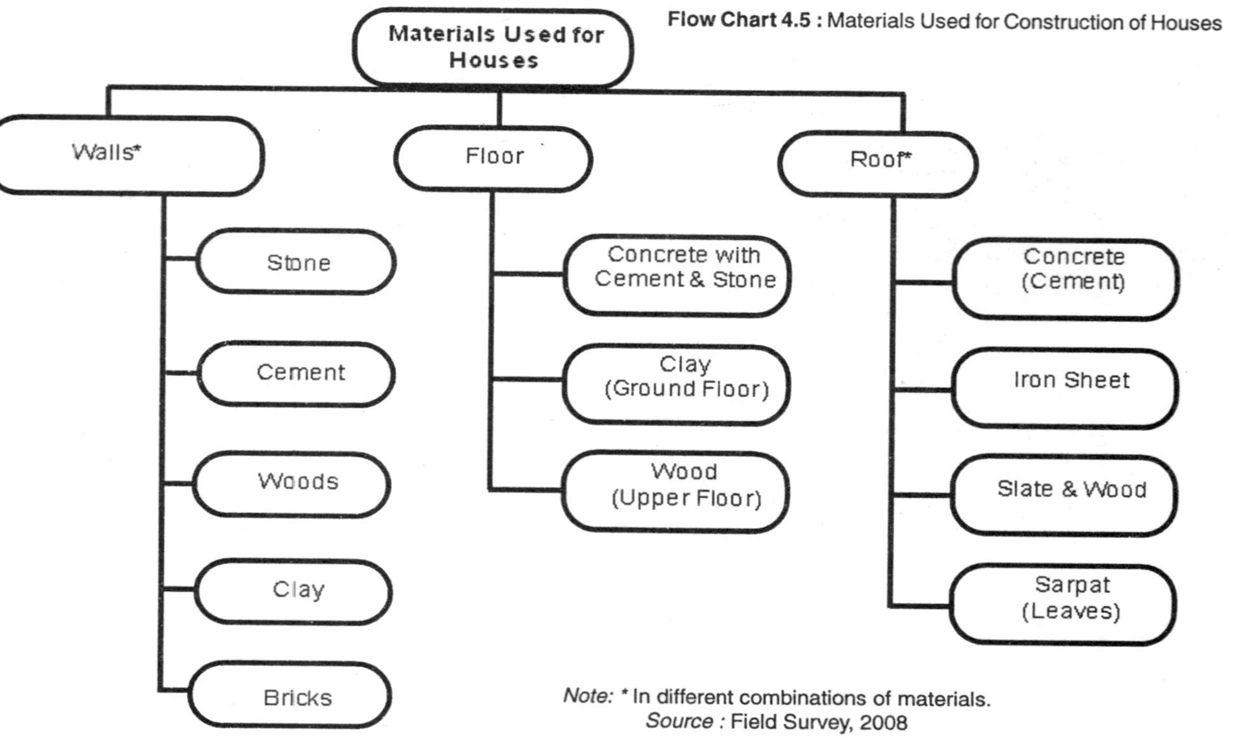

Note: * In different combinations of materials.

Source : Field Survey, 2008

4.7 Construction of Toilet and its Use

Under Indira Awaas Yojana, 65.2 per cent of the households constructed toilet that varied over districts like 94.2 per cent in Almora (maximum) and 37.3 per cent in Uttarkashi (minimum). Under Credit-cum-Subsidy Rural Housing Policy, 74.1 per cent of the households constructed toilet that was 84.0 per cent (maximum) for Pithoragarh and 58.8 per cent (minimum) for Uttarkashi. For all the schemes and all the districts covered, 65.0 per cent constructed toilet that varied between 90.0 per cent for Almora (maximum) and 36.0 per cent for Uttarkashi (minimum).

The major reasons why toilets were not constructed were 'no need', lack of money, lack of necessary water, and fund yet to be received. Of those households who constructed toilet, 82.7 per cent were in use. The major reasons for non-use of toilets were lack of water and not in habit (Flow Chart 4.6).

Flow Chart 4.6 : Reasons for Non-use of Toilets

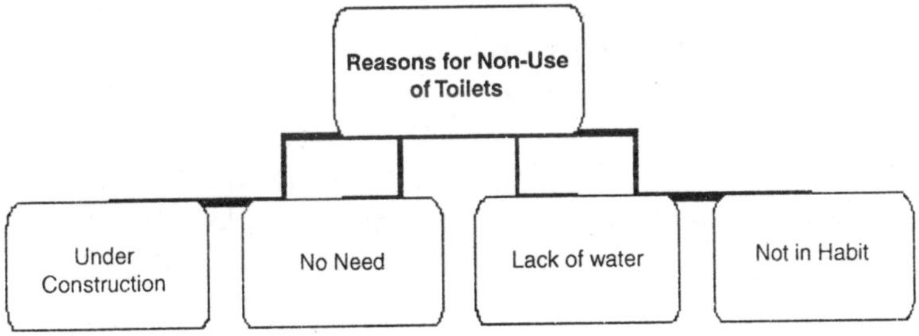

Source : Field Survey, 2008.

4.8 Use of Smokeless Stove

Smokeless stove was conspicuous by its absence in case of houses under both Indira Awaas Yojana and Credit-cum-Subsidy Rural Housing Policy and other schemes.

4.9 Modes of Payment and Adequacy of Support Money and Alternative Sources

Most of the payments for construction of house under housing programme were made through Bank Account, in case of IAY it was 85.7 per cent while in case of CCSRHP it was 67.9 per cent and in case of houses under other schemes, it was 90.5 per cent. Payment by cheque handed over to the beneficiary was made in case of 14.3 per cent under Indira Awaas Yojana, 32.1 per cent in case of Credit-cum-Subsidy Rural Housing Policy and 9.5 per cent in case of other schemes.

In case payment was made by cheque, the mode of payment was through bank account for 90.6 per cent of the households under Indira Awaas Yojana, 100 per cent in case of both Credit-cum-Subsidy Rural Housing Policy and other schemes. In case of Indira Awaas Yojana, other modes were block camp and through block officials. Overall, covering all schemes, Bank A/C was the dominant mode.

96.0 per cent of the beneficiary households under Indira Awaas Yojana, 97.5 per cent in case of Credit-cum-Subsidy Rural Housing Policy and 100 per cent in case of other schemes reported inadequacy in support money for construction of houses. In case of inadequacy of support money sanctioned and released, the alternative sources were self-saving money provided by relatives, traders, friends, sale of assets and borrowing from co-operative society (Flow Chart 4.7).

In case of households in higher income brackets (above Rs. 20,000. p.a.) self-saving as an alternative source of support income for construction of house played the major role relative to that in case of low income (up to Rs. 10,000). Generally, relatives and friends played a major role for households in case of lower income (up to Rs. 10,000 p.a.) relative to their role for households in higher income

Flow Chart 4.7 : Sources of Support Money in case of Inadequate Housing Finance

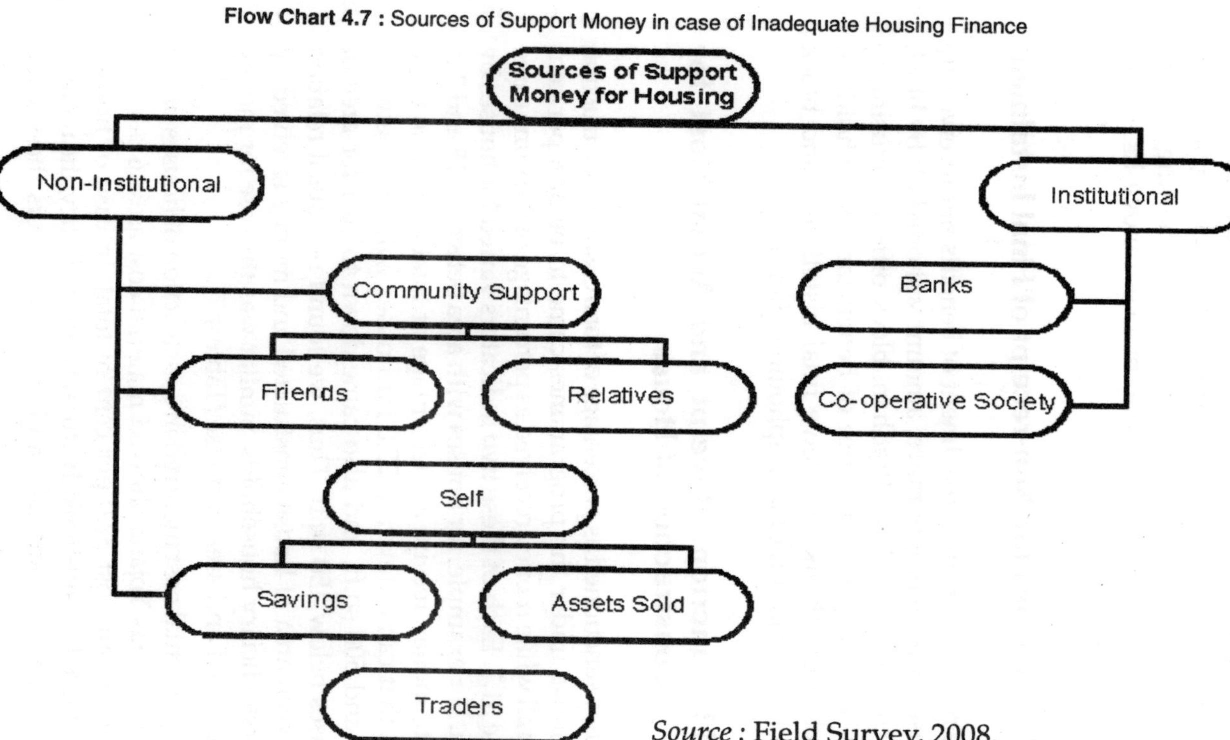

Source : Field Survey, 2008.

brackets. The role of traders was not specified to income brackets. At the lowest (up to Rs. 10,000) and higher income (above Rs. 50,000 p.a.), sale of assets did not play any role. Co-operatives did not play any role excepting for the households in highest income bracket (above Rs. 75,000 p.a.).

4.10 Reasons for Non-receipt of Final Instalment

The reasons for final instalment of benefits not received by households were ignorance, amount siphoned off by block officials and/or Gram Pradhan, block officials refusing to give pending sum, absence of beneficiary households in block office/bank to receive final installment and block officials/Gram Pradhans siphoning off money.

4.11 Sanction, Receipt and Actual Cost for Construction of House

Money sanctioned as percentage of total cost for construction of house under the programmes came to be 32.8 per cent overall while money received as percentage of the same came to be 31.1. Each of these two indicators varied for houses by area. For example, for houses with area between 215 and 225 sq.ft., money receipt as percentage of total cost came to be 40.4 that came down to 25.0 for houses with area between 300 and 500 sq.ft. and also came down to 30.4 for area of houses below 150 sq.ft. Thus, we found no causal relation between area of house constructed and money received by the beneficiary households. Similar was the case for money sanctioned and area of house (Table 4.7).

The actual cost incurred in construction of houses under Indira Awaas Yojana showed material cost as 68.6 per cent while labour cost 32.0 per cent of total. In case of houses under Credit-cum-Subsidy Rural Housing Policy, the relative ratios were 75.6 and 24.7 and in case of others these were

Table 4.7: Sanction, Receipt and Cost by Different Construction Areas

Construction Area (sq.ft.)	*Cost*	*Material Cost*	*Labour Cost*	*Total Cost*	*Sanctioned Amount*	*(vi) as % of (v)*	*Total Receipt*	*(viii) as % of (v)*
(i)	(ii)	(iii)	(iv)	(v)	(vi)	(vii)	(viii)	(ix)
Not Constructed	Cost	0	0	0	19125		17625	
	No. of HHs.	0	0	0	4		4	
Up to 150	Cost	49910	24577	73995	22500	30.4	22520	30.4
	No. of HHs.	50	49	50	51		50	
150 to 215	Cost	47371	23832	70442	24931	35.4	23474	33.3
	No. of HHs.	94	91	94	94		93	
215 to 225	Cost	46037	21104	67141	28000	41.7	27121	40.4
	No. of HHs.	27	27	27	29		29	
225 to 300	Cost	50902	24993	75275	26908	35.7	25592	34.0
	No. of HHs.	121	118	121	120		119	
300 to 500	Cost	95014	28860	123483	32968	26.7	30920	25.0
	No. of HHs.	74	73	74	77		75	
More than 500	Cost	61971	33609	95579	34529	36.1	31588	33.0
	No. of HHs.	17	17	17	17		17	
Total	Cost	58577	25520	83564	27383	32.8	26014	31.1
	No. of HHs.	383	375	383	392		387	

Source : Field Survey, 2008.

64.8 and 36.4. Overall, for all the schemes, the material cost came to be 70.1 per cent and labour cost 30.5 per cent. Under IAY, the beneficiaries on average got 96.1 per cent of total sanction, which was 92.5 per cent in case of Credit-cum-Subsidy Rural Housing Policy (CCSRHP) and 95.5 per cent in case of other schemes. Overall, the beneficiaries received 95 per cent of total sanctioned fund (Table 4.8).

Table 4.8 : Sanction, Receipt and Cost by Housing Programmes

Cost (Rs.)	*Particulars*	*IAY*	*CCSRHP*	*Others*	*Total*
Actual Cost	Materials	48680	101568	45682	58577
	as % of total	68.6	75.6	64.8	70.1
	Labour	22683	33141	25640	25520
	as % of total	32.0	24.7	36.4	30.5
	Total	70935	134278	70504	83564
	as % of Sanction	310.4	284.9	334.1	305.2
Support Money	Outstanding	0	34088	0	6835
	Received	21958	43713	20163	26014
	as % of Sanction	96.1	92.8	95.5	95.0
	Sanction	22853	47125	21105	27383

Source : Field Survey, 2008.

In case of 28.2 per cent of the households, the houses were either newly constructed in new place or constructed after demolition of old house. This includes construction of toilet. 71.8 per cent of the households got support for repair or renewal of old house, which was 75.0 per cent in case of Indira Awaas Yojana and 63.6 per cent in case of housing under other schemes. Upgradation of houses means repair and renewal of old house. In case of Credit-cum-Subsidy, there was naturally no repair or renewal of old house (Table 4.9).

4.11.1 Average Cost of Construction Per House by Area

At the peak of the hills the average cost came to be highest (Rs. 87,419 per house built) which came down to Rs. 85,410.

Table 4.9 : Houses Constructed by Households by Types of Support Received under Housing Programmes

Types of Construction	*Types of Support*	*IAY*		*CCSRHP*		*Others*		*Total*	
		No.	*%*	*No.*	*%*	*No.*	*%*	*No.*	*%*
Newly constructed at new place	Upgradation	2	7.1	0	–	2	18.2	4	10.3
	Full Support	96	50.8	43	53.8	54	64.3	193	54.7
	NR	3	42.9	1	100.0	0	–	4	50.0
	Total	101	45.1	44	54.3	56	58.9	201	50.3
Constructed after demolition of old House	Upgradation	3	10.7	0	–	2	18.2	5	12.8
	Full Support	69	36.5	24	30.0	24	28.6	117	33.1
	NR	3	42.9	0	0.0	0	–	3	37.5
	Total	75	33.5	24	29.6	26	27.4	125	31.3
Repairing or renewal of old house	Upgradation	21	75.0	0	–	7	63.6	28	71.8
	Full Support	22	78.6	12	–	6	54.5	40	102.6
	NR	1	3.6	0	–	0	0.0	1	2.6
	Total	44	157.1	12	–	13	118.2	69	176.9
Only Toilet is	Upgradation	1	3.6	0	–	0	0.0	1	2.6
constructed	Total	1	0.4	0	0.0	0	0.0	1	0.3
No construction	Upgradation	1	3.6	0	–	0	0.0	1	2.6
	Full Support	2	1.1	1	1.3	0	0.0	3	0.8
	Total	3	1.3	1	1.2	0	0.0	4	1.0
Total	Upgradation	28	100.0	0	–	11	100.0	39	100.0
	Full Support	189	100.0	80	100.0	84	100.0	353	100.0
	NR	7	100.0	1	100.0	0	–	8	100.0
	Total	224	100.0	81	100.0	95	100.0	400	100.0

per house on the middle of the hills and further reduced to Rs. 71,066 per house at the valley. Thus, as the altitude increases, construction cost rises. Overall, covering all types of houses on the three layers of the hills by altitude, average cost per house came to be Rs. 83,564 that was calculated from material cost at 70.1 per cent and labour cost at 29.9 per cent. There were variations in material cost and labour cost by area of construction and altitude of the hill that shows location of the house (Table 4.10).

4.12 Weaknesses of Constructed Houses

In case of 91.3 per cent of the beneficiary households, the house was well constructed, that was for 91.5 per cent under Indira Awaas Yojana, 93.8 per cent under Credit-cum-Subsidy Rural Housing Policy, and 88.4 per cent in case of other schemes. However, specific weaknesses were felt by households like crack wall, weak wall, weak roof. The reasons for major weaknesses cited were absence of plaster on wall, thin wall, wooden construction material eaten by insects, roof made of soil, and fear due to land sliding.

4.13 Corruption in Housing Programmes

Overall, 80.3 per cent of the households reported not to have paid bribe to get the benefits under housing programmes. In case of Indira Awaas Yojana (IAY) it was 79.9 per cent, in case of Credit-cum-Subsidy Rural Housing Policy 85.2 per cent and in case of other schemes 76.8 per cent. Mainly the secretary/block officials received bribe, partiality in case of Indira Awaas Yojana. In case of Credit-cum-Subsidy Rural Housing Policy (CCSRHP), bank officials mainly received bribe, the other agents receiving bribe were allegedly block officials, Pradhan and Secretary (Table 4.11).

On average, covering all the districts, the bribe (Rs.) paid was Rs. 3,320 for all the schemes taken together. The average

Table 4.10 : Average Cost per House by Constructions by Area and Location

Location of House	*Cost (Rs.)*	*Up to 150*	*150 to 215*	*215 to 225*	*225 to 300*	*300 to 500*	*More than 500*	*Total*
Peak	Material	58929	50829	45357	60115	102929	56667	61497
	Labour	23787	26652	21171	24146	35629	22667	26171
	Total	82715	76697	66529	84262	138557	79333	87419
Middle part of hill	Material	45333	43638	44233	50325	105111	66778	60300
	Labour	27750	20987	21327	26303	26942	34056	25588
	Total	71927	64100	65560	75978	132053	100833	85410
Valley	Material	34000	48960	52400	37132	57333	56500	48024
	Labour	13300	24774	20340	18723	28254	39370	24175
	Total	47300	72495	72740	54518	83703	95870	71066
Total	Material	49910	47371	46037	50902	95014	61971	58577
	Labour	24577	23832	21104	24993	28860	33609	25520
	Total	73995	70442	67141	75275	123483	95579	83564

Source : Field Survey, 2008.

Table 4.11: Bribe (Rs.) Paid to Agency

Officials	*IAY*		*CCSRHP*		*Others*		*Total*	
	No.	*%*	*No.*	*%*	*No.*	*%*	*No.*	*%*
Bank officials	0	0.0	6	50.0	0	0.0	6	7.6
Secretary/ Block Officials	33	73.3	3	25.0	17	77.3	53	67.1
Pradhan	6	13.3	1	8.3	1	4.5	8	10.1
Secretary + Pradhan	5	11.1	2	16.7	1	4.5	8	10.1
Patwari + Pradhan	0	0.0	0	0.0	3	13.6	3	3.8
No Response	1	2.2	0	0.0	0	0.0	1	1.3
Total	45	100.0	12	100.0	22	100.0	79	100.0

Source : Field Survey, 2008.

bribe paid under Indira Awaas Yojana was Rs. 2,776 that was Rs. 5,375 under Credit-cum-Subsidy Rural Housing Policy and Rs. 3,314 under other schemes. The average is derived from varying amount paid as bribe by number of households, that is, as a weighted average of bribe paid.

4.14 Natural Calamities, Loss to Households and Government Relief

The households at the peak of the hills were affected most (79.5 per cent) followed by those at the middle part (19.2 per cent) and valley (6.3 per cent) because of natural calamity.

The major calamities faced by households included earthquake, fire (forest), landslide, snowfall, river sliding and rainfall. Landslide was the only factor reported as a calamity in Almora, while in Uttarkashi the reported calamities were landslide, forest fire and earthquake. In Chamoli, river sliding and rainfall were not reported as calamities. In Pithoragarh, excepting earthquake, all others were mentioned as calamities (Flow Chart 4.8).

Flow Char 4.8 : Types of Natural Calamities Faced by Households

Landslide
Fire
Earthquake
Types of Natural Calamities Faced by Households
Snowfall
River Sliding
Rainfall

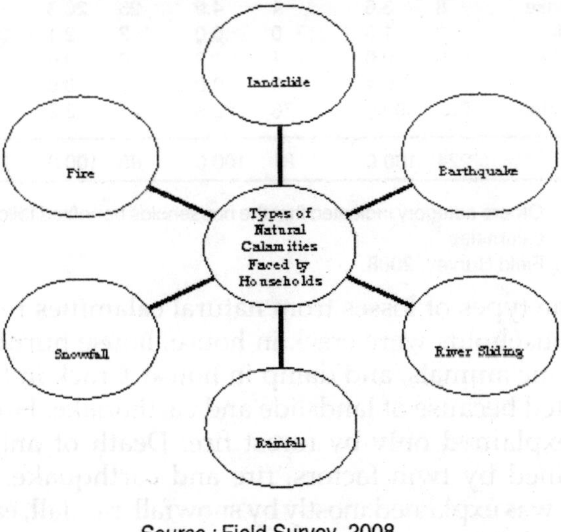

Source : Field Survey, 2008

Eighty per cent of all the beneficiary households were not affected by natural calamities and hence did not seek relief; under Indira Awaas Yojana, 90.6 per cent were not affected by natural calamities. In case of housing under other schemes, 43.2 per cent of the beneficiary households were not affected by natural calamities. Most of the affected households were affected by earthquake, fire and landslide. As opposed to claim by government functionaries to have sanctioned housing to households for natural calamities, in case of other schemes (*Bhuskhalan* or landslide), actually 56.8 per cent had been really affected by such calamities. Under Indira Awaas Yojana and Credit-cum-Subsidy (Rural Housing Policy) (CCCRHP) the selection of households was independent of such calamities (Table 4.12).

Table 4.12 : Condition of Affected Households by Natural Calamities and Housing Relief (with particular reference to other schemes)

Calamities	*IAY*		*CCSRHP*		*Others**		*Total*	
	No.	*%*	*No.*	*%*	*No.*	*%*	*No.*	*%*
Landslide	5	2.2	0	0.0	9	9.5	14	3.5
Fire	4	1.8	0	0.0	18	18.9	22	5.5
Earthquake	8	3.6	4	4.9	25	26.3	37	9.3
Snowfall	3	1.3	0	0.0	2	2.1	5	1.3
Riverslide	0	0.0	1	1.2	0	0.0	1	0.3
Rainfall	1	0.4	0	0.0	0	0.0	1	0.3
Not affected	203	90.6	76	93.8	41	43.2	320	80.0
Total	224	100.0	81	100.0	95	100.0	400	100.0

Note : * Others category indicated that the households benefited following natural calamities

Source : Field Survey, 2008.

The types of losses from natural calamities reported by the households were crack in house, house burnt, death of domestic animals, and damp in house. Crack in house was reported because of landslide and earthquake. House burnt was explained only by forest fire. Death of animals was explained by twin factors, fire and earthquake. Damp in house was explained mostly by snowfall, rainfall, earthquake and landslide.

In case of loss by natural calamities, the households got different types of relief like rebuilding house, Rs. 25,000 from Chief Minister's Relief Fund, Rs. 30,000 from HUDCO for land preparation, Rs. 5,000 for initial repair cost through Revenue Department and foodgrains.

Riverslide and rainfall did not come as explanatory factors for provision of relief. The major factors that explained relief were landslide, earthquake and forest fire. House was provided as a relief mostly in cases of landslide and fire. In case of earthquake, Rs. 25,000. from CM's relief fund and/or house were provided as relief. Thus, compensation by type and amount depended on the cause and extent of loss incurred by the household (Box 4.2).

Box 4.2 : Natural Calamities Affecting Houses and Consequent Losses and Relief Received

*Calamities**	*Major Losses*	*Relief*
Landslide	Crack in House	Foodgrains, House Rebuilt,
Fire	House Burned	Finance Support from Govern-
Earthquake		ment Departments
Snowfall	Damped	
River Sliding	Land Erosion	
Rainfall		

Note : * Most of the calamities are specific to housing under Bhuskhalan Scheme.

4.15 Linkages of Housing Programmes with Other Development Programmes

Most of the beneficiary households under housing programme were not benefited from other development programmes. Housing programme, thus, had limited impact by 'linkage effect' with other development programmes.

Seventeen per cent of the beneficiary households were linked with the benefits of other welfare programmes, most of them by National Widow Pension, Swarnajayanti Gram Swarozgar Yojana and Swarnjayanti Shahari Rojgar Yojana.

(SSRY). The other programmes that the beneficiary households under housing programmes got linked with were National Old Age Pension, National Handicapped Pension, Sarvabhoom Rojgar Yojana. The households could also link them with loans for land reform, loans for carpentry work, and subsidy for drinking water.

4.16 Impact of Housing Programme on Beneficiary Households

We calculated the impact of implementation of housing programme on the households by selected indicators. By assigning weight on each indicator and based on beneficiary response on livelihood before and after housing, we found positive impact of housing on overall livelihood of households. The percentage change in the impact under Indira Awaas Yojana was 17.2 while in case of Credit-cum-Subsidy Rural Housing Policy it was 18.9 and in case of other housing schemes also it was 18.9. In case of Indira Awaas Yojana, significant changes came via self-identity in society, respect of family, improved living condition of family and peace in family. In case of housing under Credit-cum-Subsidy Rural Housing Policy and housing under other schemes, the same factors explained most of the impact on housing of households. The only negative impact of housing in case of each (Indira Awaas Yojana, Credit-cum-Subsidy Rural Housing Policy and other schemes) was in use of public facilities. Because of housing, the households felt protected against natural calamities, and wild animals and they could assure education for their children, overcome seasonal difficulties and search for employment opportunities (Table 4.13).

The perception of the households regarding impact of housing on the livelihood of households centered mainly on safety from rainwater, shelter by having RCC roof, adequate rooms for members in family and other feelings like owning

Table 4.13 : Impact of Housing Programmes on Beneficiary Households by Selected Indicators

Housing Schemes		*Seasonal Difficulties*	*Natural Calamities*	*Social Security*	*Self Identity In Society*	*Respect of Family*	*Living Condition of family*	*Availability of Employment opportunities*	*Assured Children's Education*	*Safe from Wild animals*	*Use of Public facilities*	*Peace in family*	*Total*
		(i)	(ii)	(iii)	(iv)	(v)	(vi)	(vii)	(viii)	(ix)	(x)	(xi)	
Indira Awaas Yojana	Before	542	643	632	636	640	627	598	674	647	623	597	6859
	After	783	694	743	763	775	767	671	747	685	616	792	8036
	% changed*	44.5	7.9	17.6	20.0	21.1	22.3	12.2	10.8	5.9	-1.1	32.7	17.2
Credit-cum-Subsidy Rural Housing Policy	Before	212	229	239	238	243	237	231	246	234	237	229	2575
	After	304	261	290	286	294	287	257	284	272	220	307	3062
	% changed*	43.4	14.0	21.3	20.2	21.0	21.1	11.3	15.5	16.2	-7.2	34.1	18.9
Others	Before	261	274	278	279	283	281	254	299	294	266	256	3025
	After	340	301	344	347	351	348	307	337	314	248	359	3596
	% changed*	30.3	9.9	23.7	24.4	24.0	23.8	20.9	12.7	6.8	-6.8	40.2	18.9
Total	Before	1015	1146	1149	1153	1166	1145	1083	1219	1175	1126	1082	12459
	After	1427	1256	1377	1396	1420	1402	1235	1368	1271	1084	1458	14694
	% changed*	40.6	9.6	19.8	21.1	21.8	22.4	14.0	12.2	8.2	-3.7	34.8	17.9

Source : Field Survey, 2008.

Note : Excluded 'no' and 'under construction' cases. * Percentage changes calculated based on the following; (After-before)/before.

a house, self-satisfaction, safe from adverse weather, improved family honour.

The major indicators by which the housing programmes impacted on the households included possession of *pucca* houses, having safe house, family members getting education and employment, in spite of some households becoming indebted (Flow Chart 4.9).

Flow Chart 4.9 : Impact of Housing on Beneficiary Households

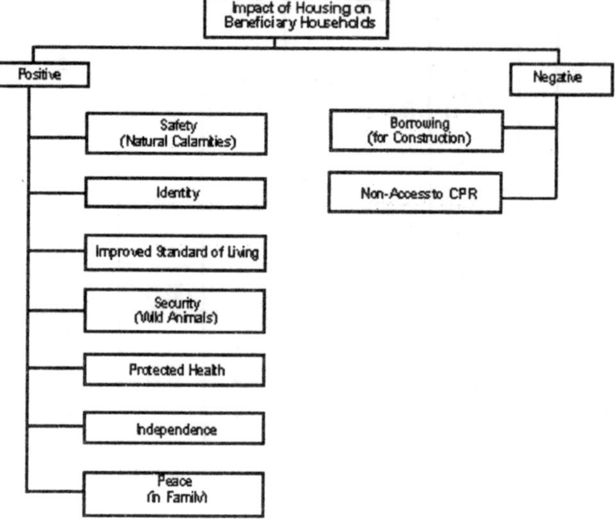

4.16.1 *Impact on Beneficiary Households before and after Implementation of Housing Programmes*

While the correlation co-efficient between selected indicators increased after implementation of housing programmes, it had exceptions for two indicators, one being uses of Common Property Resources (CPRs) and the other being employment opportunities (Table 4.14).

Each of the indicators like 'self-identity and family respect', 'security from wild animals', 'peace in family',

Table 4.14 : Impact of Housing Programmes on Beneficiary Households before and after Implementation of Housing Programme

Correlations		*Natural & Seasonal Difficulties*	*Self-Identity & Family Respect*	*Living Condition*	*Employment Opportunities*	*Security from Social & Wild animals*	*Use of CPR*	*Peace in family*
Natural & Seasonal	Before	1	.619(**)	.565(**)	.596(**)	.616(**)	.557(**)	.617(**)
Difficulties	After	1	.765(**)	.754(**)	.647(**)	.756(**)	.388(**)	.760(**)
Self-Identity &	Before	.619(**)	1	.848(**)	.748(**)	.703(**)	.723(**)	.777(**)
Family Respect	After	.765(**)	1	.908(**)	.677(**)	.765(**)	.583(**)	.810(**)
Living Condition	Before	.565(**)	.848(**)	1	.703(**)	.704(**)	.756(**)	.696(**)
	After	.754(**)	.908(**)	1	.701(**)	.731(**)	.601(**)	.806(**)
Employment	Before	.596(**)	.748(**)	.703(**)	1	.571(**)	.739(**)	.745(**)
Opportunities	After	.647(**)	.677(**)	.701(**)	1	.528(**)	.479(**)	.600(**)
Security from	Before	.616(**)	.703(**)	.704(**)	.571(**)	1	.597(**)	.580(**)
calamity & Wild animals	After	.756(**)	.765(**)	.731(**)	.528(**)	1	.281(**)	.750(**)
Use of Community	Before	.557(**)	.723(**)	.756(**)	.739(**)	.597(**)	1	.713(**)
Property Resources	After	.388(**)	.583(**)	.601(**)	.479(**)	.281(**)	1	.519(**)
Peace in Family	Before	.617(**)	.777(**)	.696(**)	.745(**)	.580(**)	.713(**)	1
	After	.760(**)	.810(**)	.806(**)	.600(**)	.750(**)	.519(**)	1

Note : Correlation has been calculated on total households (N 400) and Carl Pearson method.
** Correlation is significant at the 0.01 level (2-tailed) and status of relationship showed before and after programme.
Source : Field Survey, 2008.

'living condition' associated with housing ensured under housing programme had an adverse impact on employment opportunities. Each of the indicators had adverse impact on uses of Common Property Resources (CPRs). However, excepting employment opportunities and uses of common property resources, each of these indicators were positively linked with one another. For example, these selected indicators, have positive impact on 'peace in family' ultimately. Adverse impact of the selected indicators on common property resources may be because of shrinking space outside house, and adverse impact on employment opportunities may be because of local confinement (Table 4.15).

4.17 Suggestions for Improvement of Housing Programmes

The households suggested a number of measures for improvement of the housing programme, like increasing support money, subsidy/and provision for construction of toilet, supplying construction materials at controlled price, withdrawal of interest charged on loan, ensuring adequate target at Gram Panchayat level, stopping compulsion to construct toilet (Box 4.3).

Box 4.3 : Suggestions for Improvement of Housing Programmes

Suggestions
Increase support for construction of toilet
Increase subsidy
Panchayats should take care of all processes
Bank should mortgage revenue land paper
Loan should be interest-free
Stop bribe
Ensure adequate target as per revenue rent of Gram Panchayat by every year
Building materials should be provided at controlled price
Provision and release of single installment before construction starts
Compulsion of toilet construction must be stopped
Assistance in each programme should be same
Stop involvement of Village Level Worker of Revenue Department in programme

Source : Field Survey, 2008.

Table 4.15 : Quantitative Gaps in Relationship on Beneficiary Households before and after Implementation of Housing Programme

Indicators / Gap	*Natural & Seasonal Difficulties*	*Self-Identity & Family Respect*	*Living Condition*	*Employment Opportunities*	*Security from Social & Wild animals*	*Use of CPR*	*Peace in family*
Natural & Seasonal Difficulties	0	0.146	0.189	0.051	0.14	-0.169	0.143
Self-Identity & Family Respect	0.146	0	0.06	-0.071	0.062	-0.14	0.033
Living Condition	0.189	0.06	0	-0.002	0.027	-0.155	0.11
Employment Opportunities	0.051	-0.071	-0.002	0	-0.043	-0.26	-0.145
Security from Social & Wild animals	0.14	0.062	0.027	-0.043	0	-0.316	0.17
Use of CPRs	-0.169	-0.14	-0.155	-0.26	-0.316	0	-0.194
Peace in family	0.143	0.033	0.11	-0.145	0.17	-0.194	0

Note : Correlation has been calculated on total households (N 400) and Karl Pearson method. The gaps show that relationship decreased or increased after benefit of programme.

Source : Field Survey, 2008.

4.17.1 Requirement of Households after getting Housing Bencfits

Of the beneficiary households under housing programme, 52 per cent started thinking about getting permanent sources of income, some started thinking about irrigation facilities, some children's education, some thought to have assured water and electricity, some started thinking about widow/old age pension, and getting loans etc. Thus, households got breathing space to think about the housing related basic needs that varied for households settled in different regions in Uttarakhand (Box 4.4).

Box 4.4 : Minimum Needs Post-Housing under Housing Programmes

Needs
Permanent Source of Income
Widow/Old Age Pension
Availability of Credit
Water and Electricity
Education for children
Government jobs for children
Business Expansion
Stop land sliding/Disaster
Easy loan repayment
Irrigation facility
Land for cultivation

Source : Field Survey, 2000.

5

Role of Government in Housing

The role of the Government in housing means the role played mainly by the Panchayati Raj Institutions (PRIs) in implementing rural housing schemes through the following mechanism. First, the Zilla Parishads or DRDAs, on the basis of allocations made and targets fixed, shall decide the number of houses to be constructed and upgraded by Panchayats under IAY during a particular financial year. Second, the Zilla Parishads/DRDAs shall intimate the same to the Gram Panchayat. Thereafter, the Gram Sabha will select the beneficiaries from the list of eligible households, according to IAY Guidelines as per priorities fixed, restricting this number to the target allotted. Panchayat Samiti's approval is not required. The Panchayat Samiti should, however, be sent a list of selected beneficiaries for information.

The innovative scheme for housing and habitat development have been designed for standardizing and popularizing/replicating/propagating cost-effective, environment-friendly technologies for construction of houses, designs and materials and evolving ideal types of sustainable rural human settlements consistent with agro-climatic variations and natural disaster proneness. The Rural Building Centres Scheme is *inter alia* designed with the purpose of technology transfer and information dissemination, skill upgradation through training and production of cost-effective and environment-friendly material components. The Panchayati Raj Institutions are one of the Implementing Agencies under these schemes.

In order to assess the role of functionaries under housing programme implemented in Uttarakhand, we offered 47 representatives of Gram Panchayats, seven block level officials (BDOs) and four district level officials (Project Directors, DRDA). The role of functionaries has also been examined at the level of beneficiary households.

5.1 Role and Suggestions of Gram Panchayats

The Government of India strengthened the Panchayati Raj Institutions through 73rd Constitutional Amendments and entrusted them with the responsibility to implement rural development schemes. The Government assumed that these institutions played a positive role in implementation of rural development programmes in their own administrative zone. The Gram Panchayats happen to be the major implementing body of all rural development schemes and assure proper implementation of the programme.

Of the total functionaries as respondents from Gram Panchayats, 78.7 per cent were male and the rest female. All the sample districts were uniformly distributed by representatives from Gram Panchayats. The functionaries from Gram Panchayats were uniformly represented by castes. Of all the functionaries from Gram Panchayats, general castes were most (44.7 per cent), followed by STs (29.8 per cent) and SCs (19.1 per cent).

Most of the Panchayat representatives considered houselessness or poor housing condition as the criterion to be followed for selection of households under housing programme. The other criteria to be followed were poverty, name in BPL list, name in wait list, selected in open meetings, widowhood, physically challenged, and helplessness (Box 5.1).

Box 5.1 : Eligibility Criteria for Selection of Households under Housing Programme (As Opined by Gram Panchayat Representatives)

Eligibility Criteria

- Should be a poor household
- Should be Houseless or have poor housing condition
- Name should be in BPL list
- Name should be in waiting list
- Adequate mandate should be received in open meeting of Gram Sabha
- Should be Widow, handicapped or helpless person

Source : Field Survey, 2008.

The types of difficulties faced by representatives of Gram Panchayats for selection of households as beneficiaries include 'pressures' that the Panchayats face in the open meetings; members involved in groupism; even after saturation of SC/ST households, non-SC/ST poor households not included in the list of beneficiaries; low awareness of villagers; rules obstructing needed action; and genuine candidates often left out because of weak position (Box 5.2).

Box 5.2 : Types of Difficulties Faced by Gram Panchayats for Selection of Beneficiary Households

Types of Difficulties

- Gram Panchayat faced pressures in open meetings
- Members are involved in groupism
- SC/ST households fully saturated but non-SC/ST poor households left out
- Very low awareness among villagers
- Very difficult to work as per rule
- Some genuine candidates left out due to weak/low demand in meetings

Source : Field Survey, 2008.

Fourty Seven per cent of the Panchayat representatives were in favour of change of norms for housing (Box 5.3).

Box 5.3 : Norms that the Panchayat Representatives Like to Change under Housing Programme

Norms
• There should be no compulsion of name in BPL list • Provision of reservation in the target must change • Score based assessment of BPL household is unauthentic and has to change • Certification of BPL list must be done by GP • Permanent wait list should be prepared on annual basis • Selection of Households should be done by GP

Note : * % calculated on total number and rest % based on total wanted to change.
Source : Field Survey, 2008.

5.1.1 Households Proposed, Benefited, and Constructed Houses

10.6 per cent of the proposed households were benefited on average during 2004-07, which was 11.9 in 2004-05, 10.8 in 2005-06 and 8.1 in 2006-07. Over the regions Kumaon and Garhwal, this was evenly achieved year-wise. 92.9 per cent of the households who received benefits completed construction of their houses over 2004-07, which was 97.7 in 2004-05, 93.8 in 2005-06 and 79.4 in 2006-07. Over the regions Kumaon and Garhwal, the percentage of households who completed construction of houses was uniformly distributed (Table 5.1).

5.1.2 Reasons for Non-Completion of Construction of Houses

Most of the households (HHs) could not complete construction of houses because of lack of money. A few others could not for fulfilling other basic needs, for poverty-cum-big family size, for becoming indebted, and for illness (Box 5.4).

Table 5.1 : Number of Households (HHs) Proposed, Benefited and Constructed Houses under Housing Programmes

Year	*Regions*	*Proposed HHs.*	*Benefited HHs.*		*Houses Constructed*	
			No.	*As % of proposed*	*No.*	*As % of benefited*
2004-05	Kumaon	428	56	13.08	56	100.0
	Garhwal	315	32	10.16	30	93.8
	Total	743	88	11.84	86	97.7
2005-06	Kumaon	177	25	14.12	25	100.0
	Garhwal	268	23	8.58	20	87.0
	Total	445	48	10.79	45	93.8
2006-07	Kumaon	166	16	9.64	12	75.0
	Garhwal	255	18	7.06	15	83.3
	Total	421	34	8.08	27	79.4
Total Average	Kumaon	257	32	12.58	31	95.9
	Garhwal	279	24	8.71	22	89.0
	Total	536	57	10.57	53	92.9

Source : Field Survey, 2008.

Box 5.4 : Reasons for Non-Completion of Houses Even after Assistance is Received

Reasons

- Lack of money
- High requirement of other basic needs
- Economically very poor and big size of family
- Bank Harassed the beneficiary under CCSRH scheme Households becoming indebted after receiving housing benefits
- Illness of family members

Note : * % calculated on total number and rest % based on All Constructions not completed.

Source : Field Survey, 2008.

5.1.3 Nature of Housing Problems and Suggestions from Panchayats

The types of problems visualized by Panchayat representatives included non-suitability of houses in different seasons in the hilly region, non-ownership of land, landslide and earthquake, big family size and hence inadequate number of rooms, division of household and more requirement for houses, non-availability of construction materials, and vibration of constructed houses because of stone blasting in nearby areas (Box 5.5).

Box 5.5 : Nature of Housing Problems in Existence

Problems
• Most of the BPL households did not have adequate rooms as per the size of family • Houses were not suitable in different seasons of the hilly region • Division of family led to formation of many BPL families from a single household • Some households started living in rented house after division of family • Fear of earthquake • Sliding of land by high current of river • Houses were vibrating by blasting of hill for stone quarrying purposes • Had no land for construction of house • Non-availability of drinking water • No link road • Absence of toilet • Big size of family • Incapable to extend the housing requirement • Non-availability of construction materials near the village • Many houses needed repair

Source : Field Survey, 2008.

5.1.4 Suggestions of Gram Panchayats for Safe Housing

The suggestions offered by the Panchayat representatives for safe housing included provision of traditional type of houses, restricting construction of houses in risky locations, correctly assessing the size of household during BPL survey, increasing assistance in housing programmes, provision for safe housing, and provision for appropriate technology for housing like that of column pillar based housing (Box 5.6).

Box 5.6 : Measures for Safe Housing
(Suggestions of Gram Panchayats)

Measures
• Traditional type of houses should be provided • House must be constructed on pillars for safety • The construction of house on risky location should be avoided • Housing programme should consider the size of the household • The size of households during BPL survey should be correctly assessed • The housing target for the GP should be Increased • Drinking water should be provided • Government officials should be trained • Land disputes should be resolved • The assistance in the scheme should be Increased • Awareness among poor villagers should be generated • Safe housing should be provided • The condition of houses in rural areas should be evaluated

Source : Field Survey, 2008.

In order to improve implementation of housing programme, the Panchayat representatives suggested some measures (Box 5.7).

Box 5.7 : Improvement of Housing Programmes
(Suggestions from Gram Panchayats)

Suggestions
• Assistance should be increased for housing in hilly areas • Target for each GP must be increased by the government every year • The responsibility of government in construction of houses should be fixed • Construction of house by area should be strictly followed • Only genuine households should be in BPL list • Those households who received benefits 10 or 15 years ago but housing condition remained poor, should be re-benefited • Compulsion of land ownership should be withdrawn from housing programmes • Basic norms under housing programme must be known to Gram Panchayats • The restrictions to take sand and wood from concerned departments should be stopped • Government should not provide sand and wood at low price to BPL households for housing purpose • Compulsion of toilet construction must be withdrawn • The role of mediators and commission in the programme must be stopped • Construct house by suitable agency and then provide to beneficiary • Area of construction under housing is not suitable for hill region

Source : Field Survey, 2008.

5.1.5 Cost of Construction of a House as Estimated by Gram Panchayats

The average cost of construction of a house for a household in general came to be Rs. 58,079 as estimated by Panchayat representatives. This estimate came to be Rs. 79,000 for 'safe' construction. In case of 'general' construction, material cost came to be 66.2 per cent and the rest labour cost. In case of safe construction, the material cost was estimated to be 66.4 per cent and the rest labour cost (Table 5.2).

Table 5.2 : Average Cost of Construction of a House Estimated by GP's Representatives

Districts	*General Construction*			*Safe Construction*		
	Material Cost	*Labour Cost*	*Total Cost*	*Material Cost*	*Labour Cost*	*Total Cost*
Pithoragarh	32933	16625	49558	44286	19000	63286
Almora	42500	18400	60900	56111	23750	79861
Uttarkashi	42000	18750	60750	55460	24000	79460
Chamoli	33400	22000	55400	50000	30000	80000
Total	38447	19632	58079	52500	26500	79000

Source : Field Survey, 2008.

5.2 Role and Suggestions of Government Functionaries

Most of the functionaries in government reported that the basis of current allocation of housing targets by District Rural Development Authority to Gram Panchayats was proportionate ratio of households in the wait list of the Gram Panchayats. A few of the functionaries reported that it was based on the ratio of BPL list in Gram Panchayats and a few other reported that it was based on priority given to villages in small size population. Concentrating on three years (2004-07), the actual implementation of housing programmes following

BPL list 2002 happened mainly in 2006-07 (90.9 per cent) while 9.1 per cent happened in 2005-06. As reported by the functionaries, the basic indicators how the Panchayats selected the beneficiaries in 2006-07 were wait list of the houseless households, proposals in annual open meetings of Gram Sabha, BPL list showing houseless and *kutcha* houses, and priority given to lowest income households. The minimum support mentioned for construction of house under housing programme was Rs. 46,250 while maximum support mentioned was Rs. 70,000.

5.2.1 Reasons for Delay in Implementation of BPL List 2002

Most of the functionaries in Government reported that the finalization of the BPL list 2002 led to late implementation following the list. The other reasons cited were disputes in court for finalization of BPL identification and listing, and delay in survey work (Box 5.8).

Box 5.8 : Reasons for Delay in Implementation of BPL List 2002

Reasons
• Disputes in court for finalization of BPL List and Delay in Selection • Ignorance regarding the cut off marks for BPL • Final list has been received late from the state Headquarter • Delay in survey work for identification of BPL • BPL list of 1998 not revised

Source : Field Survey, 2008.

Most of the functionaries in Government reported that some eligible households were not in BPL list 2002 due to high score, wrong information provided to get benefits, the schedule for BPL survey did not cover the facts and conditions of the households; BPL list 2002 included non-reliability of data reported by the households.

5.2.2 Reasons for Non-construction of Sanitary latrine and Installation of the Smoke-Less Chulha

The reasons for non-construction of sanitary latrine, as opined by the functionaries in government, included inadequate availability of water to flush the night soil, low finance support for construction of latrine, need not felt by the household, lack of proper space for construction of latrine, households concentrating on the dwelling (living) unit and not on the latrine.

The major reasons cited by the functionaries in government for non-installing smokeless *chulha* were non-use for a big family by size, comfortable and useable traditional *chulha*, high demand for LPG stove, smokeless *chulha* considered non-efficient in preparation of items, and shortage of space to install smokeless *chulha*.

The gap in planning and realization is explicit in case of housing by components as shown in Box 5.9.

Box 5.9 : Reasons for Non-Construction/Installation of Sanitary Latrine and Smokeless-Chulha

Reasons	
Latrine	**Chulha**
• No need/No priority	• Not useful for large family
• No space in residential house	• Slow cooking
• Inadequate water	• Shortage of appropriate space
• Traditional habit	• Traditional chulha more comfortable
• Inadequate support money	• High use of LPG stove on top of hill

Source : Field Survey, 2008.

5.2.3 Problems of Government Functionaries for Implementation of Housing Programmes

Some of the problems faced by the functionaries in

Government for implementation of housing programme were the following :

- Shortage of grass-root level functionaries in Government,
- Eligible poor households excluded from BPL list 2002,
- Support finance for housing often spent on other basic needs,
- Division of families leading to higher demand for housing,
- Increasing cost of materials making it difficult to construct houses,
- Some agents at the village level sabotage the programme,
- Government launched the programme without ensuring skill and adequacy of staff.

Box 5.10 : Problems Faced by the Government Functionaries for Implementation of Housing Programme

Problems
• Shortage of grass-root level government functionaries • On average two or three couples living jointly in one or two rooms along with their children and show separate household • Some agents at village level sabotage the programme • Residential quarters not available at block level for village level officers, so difficult to co-ordinate them • Government launched the programme but did not ensure the skill and adequacy of staff • Increasing cost of building materials leading to difficulties in constructing the house by beneficiaries • Some eligible poor families excluded from the BPL list 2002 • Settlement of population is scattered in villages, so it is difficult to provide basic facilities to each habitation • Division of families created high demand for house in rural region • After receiving support, beneficiaries spend it on other needs • Very difficult to manage safe housing due to high probability of natural calamities • Traditional houses provide more security from natural calamities but households demand for modern house

Source : Field Survey, 2008.

5.2.4 Opinion and Suggestions of the Government Functionaries for Better Implementation of the Housing Programmes

As opined by the functionaries in government on the question of fixation of target for implementation of housing programme, the major ones are shown in Box 5.11.

Box 5.11 : Opinion of Government Functionaries regarding Caste-based Fixation of Target for Implementation of Housing Programmes

Opinion
• Reservation ratio within the target should not be fixed • Reservation Ratio must be based on caste proportion of permanent waiting list • Reservation Ratio must be based on proportion of district population • Reservation ratio should be 20 for SC and 80 for other castes • Faced difficulties in adjustment of allocation at Gram Panchayat level, if it is surplus

Source : Field Survey, 2008.

The suggestions offered by the functionaries in government are shown in Box 5.12.

Box 5.12 : Suggestions of the Government Functionaries for better Implementation of the Housing Programmes

Suggestions
• Increase the support money under housing programmes • Reservation within the target should not be imposed • Category-wise priority in housing scheme should be withdrawn • Additional staff should be appointed for monitoring • Government should construct the house, then provide to the beneficiaries • Housing Programme should be linked with other development programmes • Area specific house module should be developed • To give the right to Panchayats for amendment of BPL List • Compulsion to construct toilet and smokeless Chulha should be withdrawn • Beneficiaries must be selected by Gram Panchayat

(Contd...)

(Contd...)

- Construction of house should be done by any agency
- House must be provided by different size based on size of households
- Government functionaries should be trained on earthquake, snowfall, heavy raining, landslide etc.
- Give specific identity to benefited households and houses for future purpose
- Train the selected beneficiaries for selection of place for house, module of house and safety points
- Correct BPL survey should be done

Source : Field Survey, 2008.

6

Micro Observations on Housing in Uttarakhand

In this chapter we present the qualitative observations on housing in rural Uttarakhand. We present the observations by selected districts. We cover some individuals as special cases that reveal the problems in the housing programme.

6.1 District : Pithoragarh

As reported by the representatives of the Panchayat and the local people, while the names of needy families did not figure in the list of families who were provided housing, many affluent families who did not deserve to be given houses meant for the poor, received houses. The following reasons were mentioned by the respondents for this :

1. The survey team of the Government was reported not to have visited each household to select needy ones perhaps because the houses were situated in dangerous and slopy terrain.
2. The people believed that every year some families moved from BPL to APL status while some moved from APL to BPL. Thus, following the same BPL schedule for five years was itself inviting shortcomings in the schedule.

Case Study

Village : Malla Ghorpatta	**Name : Sri Panna Ram**
Block : Munsyari	**Age : 55 years**
District : Pithoragarh	**Caste : Lohar (SC)**

Sri Panna Ram moved to this village from village Talla Ghoomar near Milay Glacier in 1954. He was an *ad hoc* member of the Tibet Border Force. In Talla Ghoomar his house was a temporary one made of grass. He did not own any land and when he lost his job his wife left him. After his brother who lived in Malla Ghorpatta died, he shifted to his house to look after his family after accepting his sister-in-law as his second wife. At present he has two sons and a daughter. He maintains his family by working as an agricultural labourer and also rearing animals. His family was enlisted as being BPL during the BPL survey in the year 2002. In 2004 his older son obtained a job in a government school after completing his B.A. and B.Ed. and gradually his family moved above the poverty line. However, in 2006-07 he received the benefit of the Indira Awaas Yojana after being evaluated as a BPL and was given Rs. 27,500. After 2004 Panna Ram's economic condition had improved considerably and he did not need the benefit of a housing scheme. On the other hand there are many other families in his village who are waiting to obtain the benefits of a housing scheme. Maybe his improved economic condition and his increased connections enabled him to receive the benefit of the housing scheme.

3. Because the region lay in the mountainous terrain, the Government survey team perhaps could not devote much time to conduct the survey of BPL families.
4. The waiting list for the housing scheme in all the villages was based on statistics, i.e., the families with 19 points or less were put in the waiting list. Thus, many families were left out of the list.

- The Panchayats informed that prior to 2006 the prospective beneficiaries used to be selected annually at open meetings of the Gram Sabha and the names used to be sent to the office of the development block. The Block Development Office then used to select the beneficiaries from this list. Since 2006, the Block Development Office started selecting the beneficiaries and sending the list to each village Panchayat. Thus the limited power of the

Panchayats before 2006 was totally taken away after 2006, when the block development staff started directly selecting the beneficiaries. This is in violation of the guideline of IAY.

- At the Block and Gram Panchayat level the selection of the beneficiaries on a priority basis was not done.
- The majority of the Pradhans of the Gram Panchayats had very little information about the powers of the Panchayat and relied upon the Panchayat secretaries.
- The houses of the poor families were precarious by presence because the walls of most of them were constructed with stones without any joint between them and the roofs were either made of RCC or were temporary. Such houses could collapse in case of an earthquake. Both the selected blocks, Munsyari and Berinag, were in the earthquake prone zone.
- The local residents informed that the survey team of government for identifying and selecting BPL households for housing enlisted some members of affluent but large joint families with limited space in the houses as needy families.
- No information regarding the housing programmes in the blocks like the fulfilment of targets in each village each year, the names and description of beneficiaries in each category, the list of prospective beneficiaries sent from the Gram Panchayat was available at the block offices. The registers in each block for enumerating the benefits provided to the household in each village was not maintained. Thus, it was very difficult to obtain information about the housing schemes being implemented in the villages.
- Munsyari block is situated at a height of ten to twelve thousand feet above sea level. This block has a total of 85 Gram Panchayats of which 13 Gram Panchayats remain covered with snow for almost six months in a year

between October and March. During this period, the settled population comes down to the plains. These villages are situated in the icy glacier for which one has to travel a distance of almost 65 kilometers on foot in absence of any other means of transport. The villagers provided the following information :

(1) Generally, the villagers move to the lower altitudes for six months during the winter where they have their permanent residences.
(2) The sources of income of these people during their stay in the glacier are cultivation of cereals and vegetables, animal rearing, wage labour, and working as tourist guides. A few villagers who own mules carry the loads of tourists and earn around Rs. 800 per quintal for the specified distance. Some people collect and sell '*keera ghas*' (a type of grass) for Rs. 3 to Rs. 6 lakhs per kilogram.
(3) The people living in the glacier face scarcity of drinking water, absence of medical facilities, and cold weather in addition to fear of wild animals and occasional closure of roads because of snowfall and water.
(4) In glaciers the villagers can procure foodgrains from the fair price shops located in the villages in the lower altitudes. However, they fail to get kerosene oil from these shops, in spite of non-availability of electricity.
(5) In case the people living in the glacier get the benefit of a housing scheme in a village located on the lower altitude, they usually prefer to build their houses in that village rather than in the glacier. The reasons cited for this were the following:

    (a) In addition to the costs involved in carrying building materials to the glaciers it was also physically very difficult to carry them there.

(b) Most people lived in the glaciers for around six months and during this period it was difficult for them to devote their time and energy for constructing a house there. The cost of hiring labourers to build houses was also very high.

(c) No one liked to live permanently in the glaciers because of the difficult geography, intense cold, and absence of facilities like water, health, education, and means of communication. A house constructed in the glacier thus would not be livable throughout the year whereas a house in the village on lower attitude could be lived in all year round.

Case Study

Village : Kande	**Name : Jayanti Devi (F)**
Block : Berinag	**Age : 65 years**
District : Pithoragarh	**Caste : Lohar (SC)**

Jayanti Devi originally hails from Madhya Pradesh. Her husband, who was a retired army man, died 11 years back. He had two wives and after his death both his wives live together in Pithoragarh. Jayanti Devi's co wife's son works in Mumbai in a private company and they also receive a family pension from the army. They also receive some income from animal husbandry. In 1998 during the BPL survey Jayanti Devi was separately given a BPL status and in 2000 she started receiving a widow's pension. In 2003-04 she was declared homeless and was granted the benefit of the Indira Awaas Yojana. At present both the widows live together in a small permanent house with all modern facilities. The cost of the house appears to be around Rs. Two lakhs and construction work is still going on in the house.

☞ Although many people made their houses in the villages their permanent residences, they like to maintain a formal identification with the glacier since the government often granted some benefits to the villages in the glaciers.

- The targets for many housing schemes were fulfilled by distributing houses to people on a political basis. If the concerned Chairman (*Block Pramukh*), Block Development Committee happened to be a member of the ruling party and the Gram Pradhan in his favour then the targets were fulfilled easily.
- In the villages Malla Ghorpatta and Talla Ghorpatta of the Munsyari block some names were missing from the list of beneficiaries provided by the block office. As reported, usually the names of the people who had been exploited by the block office or who experienced irregularities from it were excluded from the list. The block office, however, reported that the reason for their exclusion was the change of location of these people.
- In many villages in both the blocks the block office allotted houses to people only after their houses have been fully constructed, i.e., first the houses have to be constructed and only then will the money be sanctioned. This was done more commonly for the Credit-cum-Subsidy (CCS) Scheme.
- In the Munsyari Block, the village Bhandari is inhabited by 33 households belonging to Bhotia and other Scheduled Tribes. Since 1998, this village has been experiencing tremors. The government allotted land to all the households in a nearby region but only a few families constructed their houses. The rest continue to live in their original houses in precarious conditions. During the monsoon, the administration shifts many of these families to temporary settlements inside tents in the same village. None of the villagers figured in the BPL list, following which they did not receive any benefits from the housing schemes. Most of them, being labourers, did not have the money to build houses on the land allotted to them.

- ☞ In Berinag village most of the benefits of the housing scheme had been given to the powerful Brahmins. None of these households had been affected by tremors. The names of these households also figured in the BPL list although their lifestyle was much above those living below the poverty line.
- ☞ In the Berinag, Belkot and Sagor Panchayats, many families had completed the construction of their houses before obtaining the benefits of the housing schemes. They were shown as beneficiaries and provided aid only after their houses were complete. The houses of these people had been constructed with large sums of money.
- ☞ The entire Berinag Gram Panchayat is situated on lease land, of which the families whose annual income is up to Rs. 32000 have not availed benefits of CCSRH scheme. The bankers did not sanction any housing credit to these types of land owners.
- ☞ In the Munsyari and Berinag development blocks, most of the schemes were being implemented in locations beyond the reach of the top officials because of the dangerous terrain in order to physically verify the accuracy of the schemes. The local staff and workers felt secure that their activities would not be checked.
- ☞ The money given to each family under the housing schemes (Rs. 27,500) was found to be inadequate. Even poor families were unable to construct a 20 square metre house with that money. The reasons were the following :

1. The cost of digging and collecting stones available locally was very high.
2. Because cement, iron rods (*Saria*) and other inputs necessary for construction purposes were not available locally, they had high scarcity value.

3. Since the villagers did not have access to wood available in the forests, they had to buy wood at high price.
4. The wage rate per mason varied between Rs. 140 and Rs. 170 per day and that of a manual labourer between Rs. 80 and Rs. 120 per day that seemed costly for the beneficiary.
5. Sand was both scarce and costly by its transportation.
6. Everyone desired to build traditional two-storey houses where the domestic animals would live on the ground floor and the human beings on the first floor.

- There were no facilities at any level for enabling the poor beneficiaries to buy building materials at low cost. Alongside there were no provisions for training local masons in any of the villages.
- No vigilance committees had been formed in any of the villages to ensure the smooth execution of the housing schemes. At the village level, the village development officer and at the block level the block development officer were accountable for the shortcomings in the execution of the schemes.
- In the snow-fed regions, most of the households used Liquid Petroleum Gas (LPG) for cooking either for non-available wood or available wet wood making it difficult to ignite. Wood was only used for warming up the house and for heating water.
- In village Belkot tremors occurred in 1996 that affected around 45 families, killed 10 people and buried nearly 75 animals. However, only 15 families were identified by the administration as being affected. Of these, a few were offered land who because of the unsuitability of the land did not accept it. There was acute paucity of water for both drinking and irrigation. In case a check dam was constructed for conserving the water flowing from the land on the high altitude, there would be relief

from the problems of water scarcity and the occurrence of tremors. There were possibilities of developing animal husbandry and small industries in the region but they were not feasible because of low income, low level of skill and lack of knowledge about marketability.

- Munsyari is located and encircled by Gori River with continuous flow of clean water. We found in this block no revealed crises and conflicts, no begging and theft. People here live in peace and harmony. Women enjoy dominant role in households and society for earning (often non-cash) and living. Women carry goods, fuel, fodder, rear animals, and collectively get involved in other domesic work.
- We found no revealed demand for housing as such, may be because of self-reliance, non-dependence, non-awareness about free houses like IAY, and easy availability of materials for construction of semi-*pucca* houses.
- We found mismatch between planned expenditure and actual expenditure on houses constructed, often the latter exceeding the former.
- We found strong labour market from supply side, wage rate being high in non-agricultural jobs like construction works that varied between Rs. 120 and Rs. 200 per day per worker. We observed contractor-led in-migration of hard working labourers from the state of Bihar for masonry work. Local available workers were reported to be less skilled. Also the male local workers could afford to remain without paid/productive work for a reasonable period because of female self-determined labour. Original inhabitants on the hill tops in Munsiary are confined to the locality by choice for mainly animal (ship) rearing; they are reluctant to come down to the valley even if they are provided IAY house to stay. For these settled people, animal rearing and living are the same; one household on average expects to earn around Rs. 1,000 per annum when he sells around 10 grown up sheep in

the market. People here prefer to live on the hill top even if there is danger of landslide and related disaster. People here do not expect very high standard of living and as a corollary do not expect many benefits from the government including housing.

- Market or pricing of housing materials would not have mattered much for the households on the hills had not the Government intervened through its schemes. Most of the houses were self-made through own labour and forest materials many of which were big enough by number of rooms, inside space and stories.
- Block Munsyari in Pithoragarh district remains often delinked from the rest of the state and many of the inhabitants here go to the glacier zone, still higher altitude, during some months for a different type of living. The point is that the settled households on the hills have different locations to stay for livelihood. Very rarely this relocation is under compulsion like economic non-opportunity or disaster but more often it is choice-determined. Children find schools in both the regions. One major reason for the human settlements on the hilly region in Uttarakhand remaining undisturbed and free from modernity was the non-interest of the British to permanently get settled on the hill top who colonized India for a couple of centuries as it is understood today. Even at the time of our own survey the households in the remote regions with very low population density and scattered houses showed signs of non-interest in being sufficiently modern. Rather than houses, the households were more attached to hills and nature in general. Nature being considered rich, people could share in the affluence of 'natural wealth' rather than competing for artificially generated affluence. The difficult terrains and locations for the households also obstructed them from going for 'modernity'. We found no demonstration effect and no jealousy for neighbour's wealth. In the naturally risky

zone people were naturally co-operative and minimizer of 'social distance'.

- We found 'no uniform pattern' of the houses on the hills in Uttarakhand. In some regions like Munsiary we found houses quite dispersed.
- The dispersal of houses by location had nothing to do with caste or community; it was natural selection by scope for animal rearing. Most of the households were homogeneous by culture. This homogeneity was neutral to the intervention by the government. Locally settled households are engaged in every kind of work across social categories. Economic categories are yet to get sharpened. Hence, there is social accommodation by community life and limited economic inequality.

6.2 District : Almora

Our observations around District Almora reveal the following :

- There was no Vigilance Committee at the levels of district, block or Panchayat to ensure the smooth implementation of the housing schemes.
- No training had been imparted to the masons by any governmental or non-governmental organizations for enhancing their skill and competence. The masons continued to follow the traditional methods of construction. The cost was lower in use of smooth and safe stone in construction of wall. Very few households plastered the wall by sand-cement.
- The materials used in the construction of most of the houses under the IAY were stone, wood, slate, mud, which were costly by their local non-availability. Thus, the cost of the houses was more than one and a half times the amount sanctioned under the housing scheme. The

beneficiaries usually had to take loan to cover the extra cost.

- The houses in Hawalbagh block were constructed of big stones while the houses in Salt block were made of pieces of small stones that were locally available.
- The beneficiaries had the freedom to select the location where they chose their house to be constructed. However, some people constructed their houses in places that were prone to tremors and heavy rains. The reason was that land was available only there. ·
- In the villages in Hawalbagh block the number of BPL families in the 1998 list was different from that in 2002 list. The influential people in some villages usually got the number of BPL increased so that the village would get a higher assistance that could be distributed to their own people.
- We found a number of shortcomings in the process of selection of final beneficiaries and in the preparation of waiting lists, which are as follows :

1. Since the waiting list is based on numbers required to fulfil targets, no proper evaluation of the condition of different households is done. For example, if a family has a *pucca* house then it is given full marks while it may happen that the *pucca* house may be in a dilapidated condition, water might be seeping in during the rains, it may be too small for the family, and it may be under dispute.
2. The list was formed on the basis of the survey of BPL families conducted in 2002 and was followed in 2006. During this period the housing condition of many households might have deteriorated but their names missing in the list of 'would be' beneficiaries since they were not mentioned in the BPL list prepared in 2002.
3. While forming the waiting lists of potential beneficiaries in most of the cases the views of the local

Panchayats were not taken into account. Even if the views of some Panchayat members were considered, they were not included in the lists. Thus, the present lists were totally prepared by the functionaries of the government.

➢ In view of the shortcomings of the selection process, the representatives of the Panchayats offered the following suggestions :

1. The list of BPL families should be finally approved by the Panchayat.
2. The Panchayat should have the power to modify the BPL list annually so that the names of new needy families may be added and old families who no longer need to be included may be removed.
3. The beneficiaries for getting BPL status should not be decided on the basis of numbers for fulfilling targets. Even if they are based on numbers, other related aspects should also be taken into consideration.
4. The job of surveying and identifying BPL families should be given to local Panchayats and the governmental agencies should help the Panchayats for carrying out the work.
5. The administration should not fix the number of beneficiaries at any level.
6. The selection of households for the housing schemes should be based only on the BPL list and the present housing condition.

☞ In the villages of the Hawalbagh block the houses under the housing schemes had not been constructed keeping in mind the infrastructural facilities available. In villages like Soot Dhari, Dhamas and Naula, people were suffering much for scarcity of drinking water.

☞ According to the directives of the housing schemes, the houses have to be built within an area of 20 square metres,

Case Study

Village : Bogidhar
Block : Salt
District : Almora

Name : Nandan Ram (Male)
Age : 59 years
Caste : Lohar (SC)
Occupation : Cultivator

Sri Nandan Ram was earlier a beneficiary of the Indira Awaas Yojana. After constructing the house he lived in it with his wife and five sons including Santosh, who was married and lived with his family in Delhi where he worked in a private company. In September 2007 Santosh came to the village Bogidhar along with his wife and son for a visit. On 26.9.07 there was heavy rainfall in that region which caused an earthquake. Nandan Ram's house collapsed and Santosh, his wife and his son died in it. The State Government gave a grant of Rs. 3,05,000 as compensation and also a house under the Earthquake Rehabilitation Scheme (Source – Block Development Officer, Salt). The incident that took place with Mr. Nandan Ram raises many questions which are listed below :

- Should the beneficiaries of housing schemes be allowed to select the venue for building their houses?
- Whose responsibility is it to check the durability of the construction of the house?
- Was the earlier house constructed by Nandan Ram within the standard of the housing needs of the region?
- If the region where Nandan Ram had built the earlier house was prone to earthquakes and other natural disasters, what is the policy of the State Government in this regard?

These questions are significant for the state of Uttarakhand. If these questions are not addressed, then human sufferings due to natural disasters will continue.

but no beneficiary bothered about this norm and neither were they aware of it. They built their houses depending on their requirement which was often more than 20 square metres in area and had two stories. The aid was thus less than their requirement. On the other hand, the government officials used to pressurize them to complete the construction in time. Thus, the beneficiaries often felt forced to borrow money to complete their houses leading to indebtedness.

- ☞ In one of the selected villages in the Hawalbagh block some of the houses appeared much older than the reported year of construction when the money for construction had been sanctioned. The government officials, in order to reduce their responsibility and accountability, often asked the beneficiaries to construct the houses before taking the money. It was only after the four walls were constructed, the money was given.
- ☞ In most of the villages, the Gram Pradhans were not sure of the exact role and responsibilities of the Panchayats regarding housing.
- ☞ In many villages when the sanctioned money was credited to the bank accounts of the beneficiaries, the Pradhan and Village Development Officers used to call them to the bank and ask them to withdraw the money from their accounts. The beneficiaries were then made to pay a commission between Rs. 1,000 and Rs. 3,000 immediately to them.
- ☞ In the Salt block earlier there were very few homeless families. Most of the people whose names were included in the beneficiary list were those with large family size living in ancestral houses as members of joint families uncomfortably due to shortage of space. The housing needs of smaller units of these big families were fulfilled by providing the benefits of the housing schemes. But under the new directives of the administration, genuine

BPL and homeless families had been asked to apply for the housing sanction and a new list was being compiled by modifying and updating the earlier list.

☞ Since 2005-06, the housing benefit had been raised to Rs. 27,500 for mountainous regions for the construction of a house in an area of 20 square metres. Because of the high material-cum-labour cost, no beneficiary could construct a house only with the money sanctioned.

☞ One of the directives of the housing scheme is that if the BPL score of a family for the concerned year was more than the prescribed limit, they had to give a written consent that they had no objection to the next person on the list being given the benefit. However, while preparing the BPL list no consent was obtained from the families for inserting their names in the list.

☞ The block officials informed that no technical standards were obtained from experts regarding the construction of houses, nor was there any provision for making available building materials to beneficiaries at subsidized rates. The beneficiaries were free to take their own decisions in both the cases. However, after the money was put in the bank accounts of the beneficiaries, the government officials had to exercise control on the building construction.

☞ Following the orders of Sri Rajeev Kumar Jain, Director (RH), Ministry of Rural Development, Government of India, No. 10012/2/2006-RH, dated 20 September 2006, a toilet had to be constructed within the premise of every house built under Indira Awaas Yojana. Alongside the Total Sanitation Programme had been converged with the housing schemes. In the situation where the block officials had to face great difficulty in constructing a house, they found the construction of a toilet an even greater problem.

☞ In the Salt block in many villages some enlisted homeless

families in waiting list could not derive housing benefits because of being landless also. As informed by the block officials, the Revenue Department denied existence of any landless families in the whole block. The fact is that in the official records, the male head of the family was shown to have land but as soon as his son moved out from the ancestral home without any legal entitlement to the land, he became landless. Many heads of families informally allowed their sons to get separated to help them get benefits of the government schemes.

☞ In both the selected blocks, the officers in charge were unable to provide a complete list of all the beneficiaries of the housing schemes in the last five years.

☞ The officials at the block level were not satisfied with the policies of the state government. Earlier they used to inform the problems like the sum sanctioned under the housing schemes, problems of implementation of non-departmental schemes, and problems of selection of beneficiaries. However, in spite of the information provided, there was no improvement at the state level housing scheme like the Deen Dayal Upadhyaya village housing scheme.

☞ Being a mountainous region, often a family becomes homeless even after getting housing benefit. However, they cannot be given another benefit because they have already got the grant once.

☞ Many families often show themselves as single families during BPL survey, whereas actually they are part of joint families and cook food in one oven. Thus, in many villages there has been a great increase in the number of BPL families.

☞ An SC/ST household by being a victim of a natural disaster would be given benefits even if its name was not on the permanent list of homeless people. However, a non-SC/ST BPL family will not be entitled to this benefit even by being a victim of any natural disaster.

6.3 District : Uttarkashi

The Director of DRDA, Uttarkashi elucidated on the problems regarding the BPL status of the poor and the housing condition in that region, which are given below :

1. The new policies that were drawn up following the BPL list 2002 were implemented in the district in September 2006. Thus till 2006, the BPL list prepared in 1998 had been taken as the base. The lack of coordination between departments led to a large number of discrepancies in the BPL list 2002. The exact social and economic condition of the villagers could not be captured. The villagers who obtained less than 23 points were categorized as being below the poverty line.
2. Only eighteen per cent of the people in the district belonged to the scheduled castes. On the other hand, there was provision of allotting sixty per cent of the housing scheme benefits to people belonging to the scheduled castes. In this situation it was very difficult to fulfil the targets of the housing scheme.
3. The houses in the regions of the district adjoining the Himachal Pradesh border are mostly made of wood. Just before the rainy season the people usually collect grass and fodder and store them inside their houses. This often leads to major accidents as the combustible grass and fodder catch fire, which spreads to the wooden houses. In addition, during the rainy season, there are many incidents of storms and earthquakes.
4. Many masons were being given training for a month in order to upgrade their skills so that they could build safe houses. Alongside teams comprising of local people were being formed at the village, development block and district level, who would be

Case Study

Village : Durbil
Block : Naugaon
District : Uttarkashi

Name : Sunni Devi (Female)
Age : 61 years
Caste : Pawar (OBC)
Occupation : Cultivator

Sunni Devi is a widow who lives with her son and daughter-in-law. She owns nearly five acres of land from which she earns nearly fifty thousand rupees every year. Her son earns between twelve and fifteen thousand rupees from the tourists who visit the region. Sunni Devi also owns a two-room semi-pucca house in the lower ranges apart from the three room-pucca house in the village Durbil where she lives with all her family members. The economic condition of the entire village is quite good. When an earthquake hit the village a few years ago, Sunni Devi received a house under the Indira Awaas Yojana in lieu of her original house which had got damaged. According to her, she spent nearly rupees two lakhs to renovate the house and completely modernized it. In addition, when her house was affected by the fire which broke out on 27th November, 2006, she received rupees twenty-five thousand as assistance from the Prime Minister's relief fund. When listening to her story the following questions arose in our minds :

- Is it right for a family owning five acres of land and two houses to be categorized as being below poverty line?
- Were houses affected by the earthquake that hit the village in 1998?
- Were houses affected by the fire which broke out on 27 November, 2006? How was the money received by each family as compensation utilized?

It appears that Sunni Devi used her personal influence to obtain the compensation although she is not entitled to figure in the BPL list and receive assistance.

able to provide relief to the affected people in case of natural calamities. The Department of Disaster Management had built the model of an earthquake resistant house at the district level, which the people living in the district were being encouraged to copy. However, because of the high price of the materials needed for building it, few beneficiaries of the housing schemes were able to build it with the money sanctioned to them. Because of the geographical layout of the region, it was difficult to procure standard materials needed for constructing houses at the village level. This was the reason why the villagers usually used materials that were locally available like stones, wood, slate and mud for constructing their houses that were easy to obtain.

5. Centered on the question of selecting shelterless people in the district, it was doubtful if there was even one family that slept in the open under the sky. Most of the shelterless people who were selected as beneficiaries were those who lived in joint families but the houses were too small to accommodate all the family members belonging to the extended family. These people were counted as homeless and were included in the list of homeless people who needed to be given the benefits of the housing scheme.
6. As opined by the DRDA Director, there should be no single model for the houses built under the housing schemes. The reason was that the houses built by rural families depended on their family occupation and income structure, the climate of the region, availability of local building materials, and the local trend for building houses and so on. Hence, it would be difficult to make a common design obligatory for all the beneficiaries. If the government still desired to enforce a common design for all the beneficiaries, it should construct a number of models of different

kinds so that the beneficiaries of different categories could choose the design which they wanted.

- In the Mori block the records of the housing schemes were found to be in great shambles. The list of beneficiaries of the block was unreliable.
- The Block Development Officer (BDO) of Naugaun informed that no royalty had to be paid on 150 cubic ft sand in the district. The beneficiaries often needed to purchase a large quantity of cement for constructing their houses. Alongside, if the beneficiaries desired to build their houses with traditional bricks, it was very expensive to transport it to their houses, but if they extracted stones from the mountains they would have to pay very high labour charges. Thus, the cost of the house was very high and the house itself was not durable. The BDO's suggestion was that the block should supply cement and stone chips for the construction of the houses of the beneficiaries. For this purpose at each development block four to five plants should be set up for producing cement and stone chips. On the one hand, this would help the local people to get employment while on the other, the beneficiaries would be able to get building materials at low prices, which would help them to build cheap and durable houses. He also said that in order to enable the selected beneficiaries to obtain cement and iron rods at cheap rates, the government should enter into a deal with the cement and iron rod companies so that the beneficiaries could obtain them at the block level. This would ensure availability of cheap building materials as well as employment. The constructed houses would also be strong and durable compared to the houses constructed in the traditional method followed in the mountains.
- In Mori block we found wood-made self-constructed houses on the hills that are beyond market valuation by location and beauty. In Durbil village in Naugaon block

in Uttarkashi district we found concentrated houses. Durbil village was understood to be a danger zone by being earthquake prone.

- In the Naitwar, Sidri, Mataur and Devjani villages of the Mori block most of the people preferred the traditional methods of building houses using wood, stone, slate, and tin. The store rooms of these houses were also mostly made of wood. The local people reported that the houses built using these locally available materials kept the houses safe from earthquake, rains, snowfall and wild animals, but the major fear of these houses was that they could easily catch fire.
- The government officials and Panchayat representatives at the levels of village, block and district suggested the following regarding the state-run self-financing housing scheme :

1. The target of this scheme should not be the district since in that case the boundaries of the scheme get fixed and the implementing agencies only work till the targets are fulfilled.
2. The upper limit of annual income of Rs. 32,000. should be raised so that even the slightly better off among the poor can take advantage of it.
3. The amount of Rs. 50,000. that is sanctioned under this scheme should be raised to Rs. one lakh.
4. The beneficiaries are made to undergo many formalities at the bank to withdraw the sanctioned amount. The formalities need to be made easier to enable the poor beneficiaries to withdraw money at ease.
5. The selected beneficiaries informed that the banks used to charge rate of interest between 9.0 and 11.5 per cent per annum that was much higher than they were supposed to charge.

- The residents of the villages in the Mori block adjoining the Himachal Pradesh border own apple trees from which they earn profit ranging from Rs. Forty thousand to Rs. One lakh per year. The families that do not own apple trees are involved in animal husbandry, farming and working as agricultural labourers. In the village Naitwar, the affluent people were also included in the BPL list deriving benefits of housing schemes although they already had livable houses. In this village there is a famous temple of Paukh 'devta' where a fair is held every year. Due to the influx of tourists and pilgrims to this village to attend the fair the villagers earn a good support income every year. The villagers in this block were found to usually build their houses in three parts. These are their own residence, residence for their animals, and a room for storing their essential items.
- In the village Mataur in the Mori block many families who had obtained the benefit of the housing scheme had not been able to complete construction of their houses. The chief reasons for this are enlisted below :

1. Often the area of the houses constructed by the beneficiaries was more than the stipulated area of 20 square metres. Thus, the families could not afford to complete the houses within the sanctioned aid and left them incomplete.
2. In order to complete construction, the beneficiaries incurred debt between Rs. 30,000 and Rs. 40,000 from both private and institutional sources, against their Kisan Credit Card, thus remaining unable to invest money for productive agricultural practices.
3. A sum ranging from Rs. 2,000 to Rs. 4,000 had been siphoned off from the money sanctioned to each beneficiary.
4. All the houses were made of the traditional kind (using wood for constructing the roof, floor and

walls) and the beneficiaries failed to purchase wood at cheap prices.

- In the Mori block there were many kinds of cultures and beliefs. On the one hand, the Lakha mandal perpetuated the practices of polyandry and matriarchy where women held a powerful position in society. On the other, there was the practice of girls being sold in the mountainous region in more than forty villages. In these villages there was also the practice of polygamy. The major reason for this was persisting poverty forcing women to be looked upon as commodities to be sold. Men, who had large size of agricultural land and stable business in animal husbandry and sheep grazing, usually practised polygamy enforcing gender division of labour.
- In the Mataur village, a lot of fallow and barren forest land was left empty. The local people suggested that this land should be distributed to the poor people through lease. Many families in the village received the sanctioned money for building their houses nearly one year after it was sanctioned.
- In the Mori block most of the people preferred the modern methods of building house using RCC for constructing the roofs. They did not like to use traditional methods using wood and stone which were popular there, for building double storey houses. The reason was that these houses needed extensive repair every one or two years, which was quite expensive. However, the materials needed for the new methods of building house were not easily available in that region. This was the reason why the beneficiaries were forced to fall back on the traditional methods.
- In the Sidri village in Mori block in 2003 thirteen households were affected in an earthquake but they projected themselves as twenty-eight in order to take the benefit of the Prime Minister's Relief Fund. Out of these

twenty-eight households, twenty-two families received Rs. 3,40,000 per family for rehabilitation. They spent Rs. 60,000 on buying land and the rest for construction. These families had been settled on the sides of the road and they were given the choice to select the spot to build their houses. A study of the colony where these rehabilitated families were living revealed the following :

1. Out of the twenty-two beneficiaries around ten were living in this colony. The rest were living in their original villages.
2. The place where the earthquake victims had been resettled was very dangerous from the point of view of earthquakes and heavy rains.
3. There was absence of facilities like water and electricity.
4. In order to get the rehabilitation package, each of the families had to pay a bribe of Rs. 8,000 to Rs. 10,000 to the Patwari and Village Development officer.
5. Many of the families did not get the assistance because of their absence when the patwari and other officials came to survey the earthquake affected village.
6. During the rainy season the road leading to the village becomes unmotorable and ropeways are used between Kot and Sidauli village to transport basic consumption needs.

☞ In the Sidri village housing facilities have been provided but most of the beneficiaries did not make any new construction. Instead they showed their original houses as their new constructions.

☞ In the Sidri village most of the people were profitably engaged in horticulture, animal husbandry, and in sheep rearing. While one apple tree fetched them a profit of eight to ten thousand rupees in a year, animal husbandry and sheep rearing for wool also earned them high profits. Thus the living standard of this village was quite high. In spite of this, many people were enlisted as being below poverty line.

☞ As alleged, the Gram Pradhan had kept the bank passbooks of the beneficiaries with himself.

☞ Because of a major fire in the village Devjani in the Mori block on 25 January, 2003, the houses of nine families got completely destroyed. However, to take advantage of the relief, these families got sub-divided and received large sums of money for rehabilitation from the Prime Minister's Relief Fund. The local people informed that in order to make the Patwari enlist them each family had to pay a bribe of Rs. 2,000 to Rs. 3,000 each. The families which had received the benefit of the housing scheme under the rehabilitation package of the government, revealed the following facts :

1. Most of the beneficiaries had incurred debts and the major reason was for building houses. Most of them had borrowed money from people at the village level.
2. Many beneficiaries belonging to the same family showed that they belonged to different families in order to get the benefits.
3. Many beneficiaries did not build a new house with the money received but showed their old house as having been built with the sanctioned money.
4. Housing scheme had no influence in bringing about socio-economic equality in the village. The poor people who had received housing benefits still lived in dilapidated houses while the rich people who had received the benefits by showing themselves as BPL were constructing palatial buildings.
5. The facilities that should accompany the housing scheme like toilet, drinking water, and health were

totally absent in the village. All the people were using the same source of water to get drinking water and hardly any of the beneficiaries had constructed toilets in their houses. None of them had installed smokeless stoves in their houses.

* In the Kharsari village the state-run self-financing housing scheme that was launched in 2003-04 had not been implemented properly. Alongside many people, who had been given houses under the Indira Awaas Yojana, had only used the money to repair their original houses. The people of this village alleged that the village Panchayat and the block office changed the names on the BPL list. The Gram Pradhan had enlisted his own name in the BPL list to obtain the benefit in spite of being affluent.
* The members of the Panchayat and the local people of Nanai village told that under the state-run self-financing housing scheme, the block selects a few people and sends their names to the banks after preparing their files. The banks keep these files in abeyance for years. In case the beneficiaries ask them for the current status, they are orally communicated that they have not been selected for being financed for the housing scheme. The bank officials withdraw the money from the block office under the names of these people and keep the money with them.
* The Pradhan of the Nanai village informed that the bank required a number of formalities to be fulfilled before it sanctioned to the beneficiaries under the state self-financing scheme. The Pradhan informed that the bank required a vacant plot of land to be mortgaged to the bank for providing loan to the beneficiaries under the CCS scheme. This condition prevented landless and marginal landowners from applying for loan under this scheme.

* The people of the Mori block informed that till 1998, the Forest Department used to give trees to the Panchayat at one-fourth the rate of the tree but now they give only one or two trees to the Panchayat every year. However, there was a great demand for wood in the village to build and repair their houses. The Panchayat found it difficult to decide whom to give the wood from the trees given to it by the Forest Department. The Forest Department had also imposed a ban on taking out sand from the rivers that remained violated through bribing.
* In the Durbil village of the Naugaon block in 1998, the mountains had developed cracks. The geologists had suggested that the settled people should be shifted elsewhere. The villagers informed that the Revenue Department had offered land to the villagers in the Nichla village but no one liked to move there because that region was prone to earthquake. The other reasons were that firstly their crop fields were adjacent to that village and secondly the village was close to Yamunotri, which ensured additional income for the villagers from the tourists. In the BPL survey 2002, all the 93 families living in this village were included in the BPL list. Out of these, forty one families were given benefits under the earthquake relief fund although no earthquake ever affected this village. On the other hand, in 1998 there was heavy rainfall which caused damage to many houses in this village.
* Different families affected by natural disasters were being given different kinds of relief. In the selected village Sidri, when an earthquake took place a few years ago, each family was given a relief package of Rs. 3,60,000 under the Prime Minister's Relief Fund. On the other hand, when a fire broke out in the village Devjani in the same year, the affected families were given only Rs. 22,000 under the Prime Minister's Village Housing Scheme. In

the village Durbil too, when an earthquake took place, the affected villagers were given Rs. 20,000 as relief. The difference bet.veen the reliefs granted to the three villages under the Prime Minister's Relief Fund shows that there is no universal policy of the government regarding granting relief for the rehabilitation of victims of natural disasters.

* In the Muradih village in the Naugaon block some of the anomalies regarding the implementation of the housing schemes are the following :

Case Study

Village : Kulsari
Block : Narayan Bagad
District : Chamoli

Name : Mohan Ram (Male)
Age : 44 years
Caste : Shilpkar (SC)
Occupation : Carpentry

Mohan Ram was the beneficiary of both the State Government sponsored self-financing scheme and the housing scheme for victims of earthquake. In 2004-05 he received a loan of fifty thousand rupees. Of this amount he was handed over only ten thousand rupees with which he constructed a one room house. In 2006-07 he received a benefit of twenty two thousand rupees for building a house under the earthquake relief scheme. In order to get this money he had to pay a bribe of four thousand rupees to the Village Development Officer. With this amount also he built another room in his house. He told us that he put in an additional amount of sixty thousand rupees from his own pocket. He could afford to do so as his economic condition was good. It is noteworthy that his house had never been affected by an earthquake. He is an influential member of the village and has a strong hold on the village Panchayat and that is why he succeeded in obtaining two benefits of housing schemes in two years.

1. All the beneficiaries who belonged to the scheduled castes were given the sanctioned amount in 2002-03 but each family was given only Rs. 10,000. All the houses were found to be incomplete at the time of the survey.
2. According to the Gram Pradhan for the past three years the role of the village Panchayat was negligible in the process of granting benefits to beneficiaries under the housing schemes.
3. Many cases were found in the village where the houses had been built before the grant was sanctioned.

Thus, the village Pradhan and the Panchayat, in collusion with the officials of block office, had siphoned off money from the beneficiaries at the point of withdrawing money from the bank.

6.4 District : Chamoli

Following information from DRDA and the block office looking after the housing programme in these two blocks, the following facts came to light on housing :

- ☞ Because of the natural geographical set up of the district, many natural disasters here need to be taken care of by the officials in charge of looking after the implementation of the housing project.
- ☞ There were many anomalies in the list of beneficiaries whose names were in the BPL list. For example, at the district level the BPL list compiled in 2002 was announced to be followed for the selection of the beneficiaries whereas at the block level the list compiled in 1998 was followed.

- ☞ The block officials informed that in the first phase of the implementation of the housing scheme, the homeless families whose names were on the waiting list were being given the benefit of the housing scheme. At the village level we found no homeless families. It appears that there were definitional problems with the word 'homeless'.
- ☞ There was no organizations, either governmental or non-governmental, for supplying building materials at affordable prices to the beneficiaries of the housing schemes. Neither was any step being taken in this direction by the government. Because of the hilly and mountainous terrain there was very little availability of building materials in the villages and even if they were, it was very expensive to transport them to the building site of the beneficiaries. Alongside, because there was no agency to check or maintain vigil, the beneficiaries often exceeded the amount of land allotted to them. In this situation the cost of building the house crossed the amount sanctioned to them and the poor beneficiaries had to take recourse to borrowing money at the local level, which entangled him in a web of indebtedness.
- ☞ Since the beneficiaries had been given the choice to select their own site for building their houses, many times they selected risky sites by ignorance. In the risky mountainous terrain, earthquakes and landslides caused by heavy rains led to heavy damage to the life and property of these beneficiaries.
- ☞ The allocation of a high proportion of houses for scheduled castes/tribes compared to the general castes (60:40) led to a large number of problems in the implementation of the housing scheme. Some of them are :

1. Because of the large presence of scheduled castes and scheduled tribes among the people living below the poverty line, the number of houses allotted to them soon got filled up whereas the allocation of houses for the general caste people remained unfilled.
2. During the implementation of the housing project proper records of the beneficiaries were not maintained. That is why it was difficult to get the correct information at any level, i.e., village, block and district.
3. The staff at the village level informed that because of the compulsion to fill-up the high proportion of allocation for scheduled castes and tribes at the village level, many scheduled caste/tribe families were showing that they were individual units in order to claim the benefit although they all lived in joint families.
4. Because of the compulsion to fill-up the quota reserved for scheduled castes and tribes, there was great difficulty in selecting beneficiaries on a priority basis.

- In village Kewar in the Narayan Bagar block, the BPL list prepared compiled in 2002 was being used in 2008-09 leading to continuation of priority in selecting beneficiaries of the housing scheme because their names were originally on the BPL list.
- A few beneficiaries of the self-financing scheme in Kewar village informed that even though they had been sanctioned Rs. 40,000, they received only Rs. 30,000. They were told by the bank that the rest of the money had been put in fixed deposit. However, they were not given any document of it. It appears that the bank, in order to protect recovery of loan, had put the money in its own fixed deposit.

- Another incident related to the state-run self-financed scheme came to light in this village. One of the beneficiaries reported that instead of Rs. 40,000 that had been sanctioned to him under this scheme he was given only Rs. 10,000 while the rest of the Rs. 30,000 was deposited in a fixed account in his name immediately. The beneficiary was forced to repair his old house with the money given to him rather than construct a new house.
- The residents of Kewar village reported that the money sanctioned by the DRDA was sent to the block office. However, the block office did not hand over the cheques to the beneficiaries unless it was bribed. The bribe depended on personal influence, connections, and varied between Rs. 25,000 and Rs. 6,000.
- Even for non-occurrence of earthquake in the village Kewar, benefits had been given to the residents under the earthquake housing scheme. The beneficiaries reported that they had exhausted the money given to them by the government under the housing scheme and had also incurred debts ranging between Rs. 10,000 to Rs. 15,000.
- Based on the survey of a number of villages in the Chamoli district, we offer the following observations about the construction of houses :

    1. The specified area of the house, namely 20 square metre, was not being followed anywhere.
    2. The cost of all the constructions exceeded the amount sanctioned by the government.
    3. Many beneficiary households were found who could construct their own houses without any financial help from any agency.
    4. Many beneficiary households obtained benefits from the housing scheme by displaying their original

house as having been built by funds obtained under the housing scheme.

- The rural housing scheme meant to provide shelter to homeless people who cannot afford to build their own houses is not able to fulfil its objective completely but it is motivating poor people to think about constructing their own houses. Thus in this sense, it is working as a motivational input for poor people.
- The average cost of building the houses under the housing scheme in villages Karakot and Gandik was nearly rupees seventy to eighty thousand in the village. The additional money needed for the construction was arranged for by the beneficiaries themselves. The people of these two villages were quite affluent who already possessed their own houses and they only used the benefits received from the government to extend and modify them.
- No earthquake had ever taken place in the Nalgaon village but many families were getting the housing benefit under the earthquake relief fund.
- In case the district or block level authorities desired to help a family whose name was not included in the BPL list or in the waiting list of homeless people, they used to show them as being affected by natural disasters like fire, earthquake, tremors and sanction housing facility to them.
- The Pradhan of Narayan Bagar Village Panchayat had never seen the waiting list of beneficiaries of the housing scheme of the village. Neither did he have any information about the people on the list. The officers and staff of the village development office were deliberately misleading the Gram Pradhan. In many of the selected villages, the Pradhans told that the earlier method of selecting beneficiaries through open meetings of the

Gram Sabha was much better and simpler than the present method in which the block and village level officers decide the names of beneficiaries.

- The Pradhans of the Panchayats of the Narayan Bagar and Joshimath blocks felt that the present waiting list of beneficiaries need to be amended and they should be given the responsibility to amend it. They also felt that the information collected during the BPL survey should be cross-checked by the Gram Pradhan so that only the names of eligible people are on the list. Because of inhibiting transactions cost and logistics for reaching the district and block offices a number of times, many needy people did not take the trouble and hence remained deprived of the benefits which they would have obtained had their names been on the lists by being eligible.
- In spite of no earthquake in the Kulsari village, around ten families had obtained the earthquake relief. In each of these cases the block office had taken bribes of Rs. 3,000 to Rs. 4,000. In the same village many people had received the benefit of the state-sponsored self-financed housing scheme in 2005-06 but while they had been sanctioned the amount of Rs. 50,000 each, they had received only Rs. 10,000 each. None of them had any information about the rest of the money.
- In the Salaar Dugra village in the Joshimath block an earthquake in 1999 affected the houses of thirty four households. Out of them twenty families were given benefit of housing under the earthquake relief scheme. In addition, the Revenue Department gave each family between Rs. 10,000 and Rs. 25,000 depending on the extent of damage to their houses. However, the villagers failed to say what the money was used for. At present almost all the people are living in their old houses which they have repaired. The other fourteen families who did not receive the benefit of the housing scheme are still

waiting to get assistance for building their houses. The village is still prone to earthquakes. The major reason for stay is that the agricultural lands owned by the villagers are close to these places.

- In the Merang village, the bank was charging an interest rate of 12.5 per cent per annum from the beneficiaries of the state-sponsored self-financing housing scheme that caused resentment among the beneficiaries.
- In the revenue village Paing, village Panchayat Reri, under the Joshimath block, the earthquake which had occurred in 1999 had caused cracks in the houses of forty eight families. Earthquakes and tremors are regular occurrences in this region and this is why twenty of these forty eight families have been settled in Adarshnagar Daggural, thirty five from Joshimath. Along with the benefit of the housing scheme, thirty three families have been given a benefit of Rs. 30,000 each by HUDCO for levelling their land. HUDCO has adopted this village but because of the problems affecting the village due to geographical reasons it has only donated money to the villagers. The Revenue Department of the State Government donated between one and twenty-five thousand rupees to each of the forty-eight families from natural disaster fund. Adarshnagar, where the earthquake affected families had been rehabilitated, all twenty families had constructed their houses there but only four were living there permanently. The rest were still living in their original village. The reason why these families did not like to live in the new village was that there was no agricultural land nearby, there was no forest for gathering fodder for their animals, there was no electricity connection there and there was only one source of drinking water in the village for all the residents.

6.5 Need Assessment of Rural Society in Uttarakhand

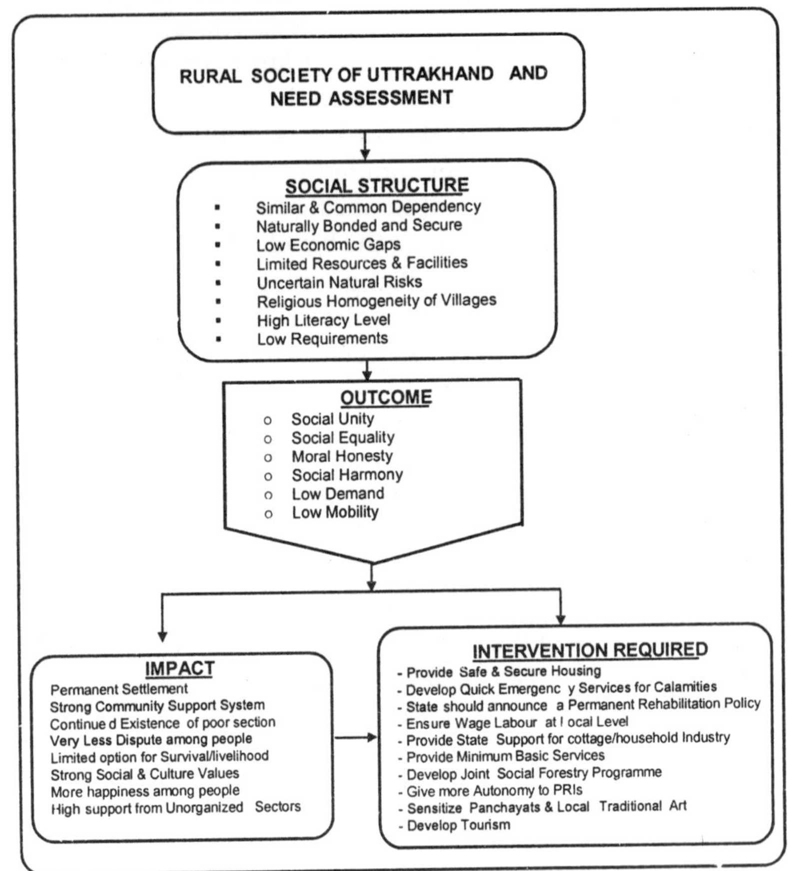

7

For Decent Housing on the Hills

Rural housing as a means of living ensures not only safe and comfortable living of the rural population, but also stops forced migration of people. The employment response of planned rural housing and its positive links with other development schemes may retain rural population within the rural region. An income-poor family can afford to spend an insignificant proportion of its income on housing, if at all, after money is spent on other basic needs of life like food and clothing. Money spent on housing is lump sum at a particular point of time while money spent on food is regular. In rural society in India nobody lives without food on a long time span while one may live without owning a house over years. This is because of the lowest cost coverage below which a minimum necessary housing provision cannot be ensured. If there is a sizeable section of the rural population who is income-poor, then low-cost rural housing is one of the means of social security for them. Low-cost rural housing uses local raw materials available often free of cost and manpower for such constructions. The utilization of local manpower may also signal if there had been any diffusion of technology through Government initiatives in constructing houses. Investment in housing by the Government for the income-poor families can improve the living and working conditions of low-income families, stop forced migration by increasing the opportunities for local employment by linkages with other development schemes of the Government and stimulate the development of other sectors of the economy. This occurs by safe existence and stability of the households via housing and optimizing the time in productive uses. Planning for rural housing by uses of local materials, labour and credit shows the avenues for not only the utilization of local resources that otherwise would have remained idle, but also saving scarce resources of the economy for alternative uses.

7.1 Settlement, Migration and Relocation of Households

Almost all the households were settled in rural Uttarakhand by birth. Very few who used to migrate did so to get support income. Absence of employment opportunities was the most important reason for migration. The other reasons included absence of educational institutions and unwelcome relations with neighbours in the locality.

A significant percentage of all the households had double settlement. The relocation occurred mostly from the peak of the hills. The major reasons for double settlement were snowfall by being a major problem and cultivation by offering economic opportunities. This is different from the conventional 'push' and 'pull' factors for migration. This double settlement is choosing between altitudes as alternative settlements on hills.

Most of the relocated households who owned the second house relocated them for cultivation, wage-labour, weaving/ sewing, animal husbandry and business. They earned adequate support income from the second settlement.

In the second location of the relocated households, the major problems faced were non-availability of water and electricity, followed by less employment opportunity and difficulty in getting foodgrains from FPSs. The scarcity of water and electricity was felt most on top of hills, where half of the households used to get re-relocated for a period of five to six months per year. The rest half used to re-settle on the middle of the hills and valley.

Almost all the beneficiary households selected their own location for construction of houses. Most of the houses were in traditional module, which revealed the local choice of the households. The reasons why some of the completely constructed houses were not being used were inadequate space, absence of required facilities, long distance from village/main habitation and insecure place. The reasons why houses remained under construction were shortage of finance, death of family member, difficulties in making materials available. Division of family led to transfer of houses.

7.2 Mode of Payment and Receipt of Money for Housing

Most of the payments for construction of house under housing programme were through Bank Account.

Most of the beneficiary households reported inadequacy in aid provided for construction of houses. In case of such inadequacy, the other sources were self-saving, money provided by relatives, traders, friends, sale of assets (land, animals etc.), and borrowing from cooperative society.

In case of households in higher income brackets (Rs. 20,000. p.a. and above) self-saving as a support money for construction of house played the major role relative to that in case of households with low income (up to Rs. 10,000.). Generally, relatives and friends played a major role for households in case of lower income (up to Rs. 10,000. p.a.) relative to their role for households in higher income brackets.

7.3 Cost of Housing

Overall, for all the schemes, the material cost came to be 70.1 per cent and labour cost 30.5 per cent of total cost for construction of a house under the housing schemes.

At the peak of the hills the average cost came to be highest (Rs. 87,419 per house built) which came down to Rs. 85,410. per house on the middle of the hill and further reduced to Rs. 71,066 per house at the valley. Thus, as one goes up in altitude, construction cost rises. Overall, covering all types of houses on the three layers of the hills by altitude, average cost per house came to be Rs. 83,564 composed of material cost at 70.1 per cent and labour cost at 29.9 per cent.

The difficult transport and hence high cost of materials like bricks, cement, iron and stone chips on the high altitude may be a major limiting factor for construction of *pucca* houses. *Pucca* houses also seem not enough to resist the natural disasters like earthquake and landslide. In this case, there are reasons for the households not to spend much on *pucca* houses.

7.4 Impact of Housing

The households at the peak of the hills were affected most by natural calamity followed by those at the middle part and valley. The major calamities faced by households included earthquake, fire, landslide, snowfall, river sliding and rainfall. Crack in house was reported because of landslide and earthquake. House burnt was explained only by domestic fire. Death of animals was explained by fire and earthquake. Falling down of house was explained mostly by snowfall, rainfall, earthquake and landslide.

We found positive impact of housing on overall

livelihood of households. Through housing significant changes came via self-identity of individuals in society, respect of family, improved living condition of family and peace in family. The only negative impact of housing was in use of public facilities. Because of housing, the households felt protected against natural calamities and wild animals. Because of housing, they could save money for the education of their children, overcome seasonal difficulties and search for employment opportunities. State-provided housing, however, had adverse impact on uses of Common Property Resources (CPRs). The perception of the households regarding impact of housing on the livelihood of households centered mainly on safety from rainwater, shelter by having RCC roof, adequate rooms for members in family and other feelings like owning a house, self-satisfaction, safety from adverse weather, and improved family honour.

The people living in the glacier also prefer to build their houses in low altitude rather than living in the glacier. The reasons cited were the following :

(a) In addition to the costs involved in carrying building materials to the glaciers it was also very difficult to carry them there.
(b) Most people lived in the glaciers for around six months and during this period it was difficult for them to devote their own time and energy for constructing a house there. The cost of hiring labourers to build houses was also very high.
(c) No one liked to live permanently in the glaciers because of the difficult geography, intense cold, and lack of infrastructural facilities like water, health, education, and means of communication.

The houses on the hills in Uttarakhand had 'no uniform pattern' and location. In the remote hills, most of the households were homogeneous by culture. Not much intervention by the government so far helped maintain this homogeneity. Locally settled households were engaged in every kind of work across social categories. Economic categories were yet to get sharpened. Hence, there was social accommodation by community life and limited economic inequality.

7.5 Suggestions for Decent Housing by Catalysts

Suggestions from Households

- The households suggested increasing support money under IAY, increasing subsidy in CCS, increasing provision for construction of toilet, supplying construction materials at controlled price, interest-free loan, ensuring adequate target at Gram Panchayat level, and eliminating compulsion to construct toilet.
- Most of the beneficiary households started thinking about getting permanent sources of income, irrigation facilities, children's education, assured water and electricity, widow/old age pension, and loans. Thus, the households got breathing space to think about fulfilling the housing-related basic needs once they got houses.

Suggestions from Panchayat Representatives

- The Panchayat representatives suggested that there should be no compulsion for the name of the households to be in the BPL list to get housing, that the provision of reservation in the target has to change, that the wait list has to be prepared on an annual basis, that the selection of households and certification of BPL list should be done by Gram Panchayat.

- The types of problems visualized by Panchayat representatives included non-suitability of houses in different seasons in the hilly region, non-ownership of land, landslide and earthquake, big family size and hence inadequate number of rooms, division of household and requirement for more houses, non-availability of construction materials, and vibration of constructed houses because of stone blasting in nearby areas.

Suggestions from Government Officials

The government officials suggested the following regarding the state-run self-financing housing scheme :

1. The target of the housing scheme should not be the district since in that case the boundaries of the scheme get fixed and the implementing agencies only work till the targets are fulfilled.
2. The prevailing upper limit of annual income of Rs. 32,000 should be raised so that the less poor can take advantage of it.
3. The modus operandi to withdraw the sanctioned aid from the bank should be made easier for the beneficiaries.
4. The government should ensure that the banks charge reasonable rate of interest on loans for credit-cum-subsidy scheme.

7.6 Towards Decent Housing

While construction of house and living in privately owned house remain a private domain, the location of the house shows space under the jurisdiction of the state. Hence, apart from provision of houses for the income-poor, the state may have reasons to intervene in housing by planning and settlement of households and relocation if and when necessary. Based on our observations, we recommend the following for decent housing :

- Households should be prevented from constructing their houses in dangerous places like earthquake-prone zones. There has to be a sensible rehabilitation policy in case a particular zone is declared earthquake-prone where people are already settled. This will be the responsibility of the State Government.
- No housing for settlement of households should be allowed above 15,000 ft. for natural safety of the households and protection of nature. The hilly zone above this specified height should be the 'natural zone' reserved/preserved by the state.
- The argument for *pucca* (concrete) house generally may not be the only solution for living by households on the hills at different altitudes. The type of the house on the range of hills will depend more on the climatic conditions and natural slopes than on the conventional indicators like safety and security.
- Often the semi-*pucca* houses made of wood and boulder as components of wall, tin/slate as component of roof, and clay for floor may be more acceptable and climate-friendly for the households relative to conventional concrete (*pucca*) houses. The choice has to be left to the households for these components of house.
- The roof of the residential house preferably will be conic in case it is located on the top because of snow fall while it may be flat when the altitude at which

the house is located is much lower. On the areas adjacent to dense forests, the house has to be more than one-storey building to remain protected from wild animals while at the bottom of the hills it may be single storey depending on the requirement of family members and domestic animals.

- In case the target households own land where they construct residential house, the state has to look into the general drainage and sewerage system before allowing construction of the house under the housing schemes. In case the target households like the widow of military personnel killed in war, and physically challenged persons do not own land, the location has to be decided by the state in agreement with the beneficiary household, so as to ensure public facilities like water, electricity, drainage and sewerage, health-related facilities, educational institutions, transport, and market.
- Following the natural voluntary division of the large household into a number of nuclear families, the right to being enlisted in BPL should not be automatically ensured. In such cases, the offshoot nuclear household may be suggested to go for credit-cum-subsidy scheme.
- The fixed norm of 20 sq. mt. as construction area has to be relaxed depending on the altitude, transportation cost and availability of natural safe space.
- The implementing authorities should guide the target households to use local materials and cost-effective disaster resistant and environment-friendly technologies. The implementing authorities should contact organizations and institutions for information on suitable building materials, designs and methods to help the households in the construction of durable and cost-effective houses. This will also lead to

training-cum-information sharing of the households considered as beneficiaries under housing.

- The basic information like BPL list, permanent wait list of households for housing programme, list of disaster-resistant construction, Family Register, details of households who benefited by other development programmes must be available in each Gram Panchayat office.

7.7 Catalysts of Execution

The catalysts for execution of policies for decent housing are the institutions within the general frame of the state. For rural region, these institutions mostly cover the PRIs.

The Gram Panchayat has to take following steps :

(i) Certify the BPL list prepared by the competent authority and has to follow the list while selecting households as target beneficiaries,

(ii) Convene open meetings of Gram Sabha and enlist names of shelterless households, widows, physically and mentally challenged people, in addition to the pre-fixed quota for SCs and STs,

(iii) Organize awareness campaign each year so far as construction of houses is concerned for the safety and security of the households, and

(iv) Prepare permanent wait list on an annual basis and send it to Block office and DRDA for their acceptance.

In addition, the Panchayat should include poor non-SC/ST households in case the region does not have adequate number of SC/ST households. The Panchayat has to assess every year the condition and durability of the houses constructed under housing schemes and suggest measures accordingly for upgradation of the house and guide the households for temporary relocation. The Panchayat should take the responsibilities for marketing of local agro-based, forest-based and household industry products produced by income-poor household-entrepreneurs, particularly women, to provide them support income. In case of forestry-based products, there has to be a joint responsibility by a trio : the entrepreneur-household, the Gram Panchayat and the Forest Department to ensure participation in replenishment of forestry on a planned time span, once forest resources are allowed to be converted into individual products. The Gram Panchayats should promote construction of traditional houses that we found more acceptable to the households without any compromise with safety and security of the households. The Gram Panchayat should enlist the permanent address of the specified households in case of double settlement of households on the hills.

In case of landless, assetless and incomeless households, Gram Sabha land has to be provided for their housing and compulsion of land ownership has to be withdrawn from housing schemes.

The State Government has to allow the beneficiary households to take sand and wood from the concerned departments at subsidized rates.

Since, the Panchayats so far played a significant role in all the housing schemes, hence the state Government has to strengthen the PRIs by assigning them more rights and responsibilities like organizing awareness programmes regarding safe housing, monitoring and supervision of implementation of the housing schemes.

The State Government has to link housing schemes with other on-going welfare-cum-development schemes in the state.

The State Government should develop and launch an integrated training programme for representatives of Gram Panchayats and settled households that have to cover all aspects of disaster management.

The State Government should empower Gram Panchayats with amending the permanent wait list in its jurisdiction on an annual basis. Provision of reservation should be based on ratio of caste/class of permanent wait list or the number of BPL households in the Gram Panchayats.

The State Government should develop 'model house' based on location, tradition of the locality, household requirements, safety and security, climate and calamity. The enlisted and selected households should be given the choice to select one model from the module box following which the money will be sanctioned.

The government has already made the provision of supplying construction materials to beneficiary households at controlled price. However, based on our non-observation of any household availing this facility and also based on high transport cost on the hills, the responsibility of arranging construction materials for sale at subsidized prices at a particular zone has to be ensured by the block level officials.

In view of the cheap usable cement blocks for construction of walls defining perimeter of the house by plinth area, the use by more of such techniques by other households should be encouraged by the government. The responsibility for dissemination of this knowledge has to be executed through the block officials or NGOs/SHGs and supported by the GP.

The State Government has a regular policy of rehabilitating households in distress following natural calamities that has to continue by schemes like Prime Minister's Relief Fund, and State Relief Fund.

The State Government has to form vigilance committees at multiple levels like village, block and district to look into the grievance of the households that they may face in getting their names enlisted for housing benefits up to getting money released for the said purpose. The details about this committee by names of members and assigned duties have committee by names of members and assigned duties have to be displayed in public places and a register maintained by the concerned office for redressal of grievances.

The construction of private toilet for use should not be a part of housing programme. The question should be left to Total Sanitation Programme.

The installation of smokeless stove as an integral component of IAY should be withdrawn. Instead, the government should provide option to beneficiary households to take LPG connections at subsidized rate for the hills.

Since wood happens to be the main fuel for the households on the hills, hence, there has to be replenishment of wood as a source of fuel by joint forest management approach rather than stopping the households from using wood as a fuel for cooking.

All the concerned officials in the Government should be made aware of the rule that the Gram Sabha is the final authority for selection and approval of the beneficiary and that no further approval is required by any other authority.

Generally, CCS scheme fails when the IAY offers 'money gift' for housing. The not-so-poor also do not have much idea about the CCS scheme. This awareness may be generated by the Panchayat/state government so that the households above the margin or in the wait list with remote chance to get IAY house in the foreseeable future may be persuaded to go for CCS scheme. The banking services for CCS have to be easy to encourage the households to opt for it. Each Gram Panchayat must have one bank with loanable fund to assist in execution of CCS scheme.

Based on our observations on housing for living in rural Uttarakhand, we are convinced that not much state intervention is warranted there unless natural calamities make the households shelterless. In case of calamities of varied nature, enlistment of poor households once will not be enough. Housing requirement in hilly region in rural Uttarakhand thus require intervention of a type different

Bibliography

Census of India, 1981, 1991, and 2001, Population Series.

Census of India, 2001, Series-I.

Government of India, 1996, September, Draft Mid-Term Appraisal of the Eighth Five Year Plan, 1992-97, Planning Commission, New Delhi.

Government of India, Ministry of Finance, Economic Survey, 1993-2000.

Government of India, Planning Commission, First Five Year Plan to Eighth Five Year Plan, New Delhi.

Government of India, Planning Commission, Ninth Five Year Plan, 1997-2002, Vol. II, New Delhi.

Government of India, Planning Commission, Tenth Five Year Plan, 2002-07, Vol. II, New Delhi.

Government of India, Planning Commission, Eleventh Five Year Plan, 2007-2012, Vol. III, New Delhi.

Government of Uttar Pradesh, 1997, State Planning Commission, Draft Ninth Five Year Plan (1997-2002), Vol. 1, October, Lucknow.

Government of Uttar Pradesh, Planning Department, Seventh Five Year Plan, A Framework (1980-85), Lucknow.

Government of Uttar Pradesh, State Planning Commission, 1994, Annual Plan, 1994-95, Vol. I, Lucknow.

Hodge, Ian and Whitby, Martin, 1981, *Rural Employment, Trends, Options, Choices*, Methuen, London.

Kumar, Shalini, n.d., External Intervention in Rural Building

Process, Dissertation Submitted to the School of Architecture, Ahmedabad (unpublished).

Mathew, George, 'Local Self-Government and the PACS States', at the national seminar on 'Advocacy for Realizing Rights and Eradicating Poverty', organized by the PACS Programme in New Delhi, January 30-31, 2004.

National Human Development Report, 2001, Planning Commission, Government of India.

Sarvekshaana Vol. XXII no. 3, 78 issue, 1999 published by NSS Organization, Department of Statistics, Government of India.

Task Forces on Housing and Urban Development, Shelter for Urban Poor and Slum Improvement, Septemebr 1983, Planning Commission, Government of India.

United Nations, 1978, Department of Economic and Social Affairs, 'The Significance of Rural Housing in Integrated Rural Development' (Report of the Ad Hoc Group of Experts on the Significance of Rural Housing and Community Facilities in Integrated Rural Development), New York.

Wakely, P.I., Schmetzer, H., and Mumtaz, B.K., 1976, '*Urban Housing Strategies, Education and Realization*', Pitman Publishing, London.

Index